Technology-Based Learning:

A HANDBOOK FOR PRINCIPALS AND TECHNOLOGY LEADERS

Technology-Based Learning:

A HANDBOOK FOR PRINCIPALS AND TECHNOLOGY LEADERS

by
Tweed Wallis Ross, Jr.
and
Gerald D. Bailey

SCHOLASTIC

LEADERSHIP
POLICY
RESEARCH ™

NEW YORK • TORONTO • LONDON • AUCKLAND • SYDNEY

ISBN 0-590-49626-3

12 11 10 9 8 7 6 5 4 3 2 1   5 6 7 8 9/9

Printed in the U.S.A.

Library of Congress Cataloging-in-Publication Data

Ross, Tweed Wallis, Jr.
   Technology-based learning: a handbook for principals and technology leaders /
   by Tweed Wallis Ross, Jr., Gerald D. Bailey.
       p.   cm.
   Includes bibliographical references.
   ISBN 0–590–49626–3
   1. Educational technology.   2. Computer-assisted instruction.   3. Learning.   4. Educational leadership.
   5. Educational change.
I. Bailey, Gerald D.   II. Title.
LB 1028.3.R67   1995
371.13'078—dc20   94–212518
                                                                            CIP

TABLE OF CONTENTS

ACKNOWLEDGMENTS

In writing this book, the authors have incurred the debt of a legion of friends. The errors and omissions remain with the authors, but much of the substance of the book comes from the diligent work of a large number of practitioners in the field of education. These practitioners willingly donated their time and expertise. Through their thorough review and helpful comments, the principals, educators, and technology specialists who aided in the field test of this handbook added much to the content.

We wish to thank our colleagues and fellow collaborators at Kansas State University. Their support and encouragement have been unflagging. Without their insight and intuition this handbook would never have come to print.

As always, our professional debt is to our closest colleagues, who are also our wives—Maxine and Gwen. Without their support, decency, rationality, and encouragement, publication would be a task whose burdens were far beyond the emotional rewards. Finally, a special note of thanks is reserved for Dr. Gwen Bailey. Her tireless proofreading efforts hammered this document into a manageable form. Dr. Bailey's efforts in correcting both trivial and substantive errors were incalculable.

Tweed W. Ross, Jr. and Gerald D. Bailey
1995

INTRODUCTION

KEY QUESTION

Why this handbook?

Building principals are challenged to be agents of educational change. Principals find time, energy, and commitment stretched to unreasonable limits. American educational practices have placed heavy burdens on the principalship in a time when principals are swimming in a sea of demands for change. This sea of demands seethes with calls for reform, restructuring, and transformation. Emerging technologies are central to many of these change efforts. Principals find it difficult to muster the energy and time to grasp new learning patterns generated by emerging technologies. This book provides principals with a framework for using technology to enhance student learning.

Principals need a definition of *reform*, *restructuring*, and *transformation*. In the general sense, "restructuring asks individuals at all levels of the educational system to change the way they think about and do their jobs" (David, 1991, p. 39). This handbook focuses on the technology-based learning methods. Current change efforts differ from earlier attempts in two ways: 1) they are driven by challenging goals for student learning, and 2) they call for systemic change of the educational system at all levels (David, 1991). To that extent, this principal's handbook recognizes that technology is not the only factor involved in educational change. However, technology is a core aspect of educational change. Without making effective use of emerging technologies in the learning process, change efforts will be incomplete.

KEY QUESTION

What does this handbook do for principals?

The purpose of this handbook is to give building principals a working document that allows them to be leaders in helping teachers create technology-based learning methods. Often, when dealing with emerging technologies in the educational process, principals are left with puzzling questions.

PREFACE

1

Why are we planning?

Where is all this leading?

Where does it all fit in the school business?

What am I getting into?

This handbook enables principals to frame answers to these questions. The handbook is designed for principals who are interested in using technology to alter their school's educational process but are neither experts, nor wish to become experts in technology. Often, technology planning activities provide the means without establishing the goals for new methods of instruction. *Technology-Based Learning* helps principals define the goals of technology planning efforts. This handbook also responds to the needs of technology experts who are creating new ways to use educational technology to enhance the learning process. This handbook empowers principals and technology leaders in seven specific ways.

- ◆ The handbook provides background for understanding the principal's role in changing to Information Age learning.

- ◆ The handbook provides a model for developing and adopting new technology-based learning methods.

- ◆ The handbook provides resources to use in developing and explaining new technology-based learning methods.

- ◆ The handbook provides technology leaders with information that helps frame their role in changing environments while furnishing resources and models for understanding technology's role in the rapidly changing learning process.

- ◆ The handbook provides goals for technology planning efforts.

- ◆ The handbook provides limited recommendations for specific brands without being committed to a particular platform or corporation.

- ◆ The handbook enables principals to communicate learning goals with network administrators, software engineers, technicians, and technology coordinators.

In summary, this handbook helps principals and technology leaders exercise a leadership role in implementing technology-based learning methods in their schools.

KEY DEFINITIONS

Certain terms used throughout this book are crucial to a conceptual understanding of our meaning. These key definitions have been inserted here to establish clarity for the readers and help them understand our categorization of technology-based learning methods.

EMERGING TECHNOLOGIES

Emerging technologies are a general class of electronic learning tools, usually based on digital technologies, that are having a major impact on information manipulation, distribution, and communication. These technologies include LCD panels, micro-computers, computer networks, television, modems, videodisc, CD-ROM, satellite, software, etc.

BUILDING PRINCIPAL

Building principal refers to the individual charged with the educational curriculum, building administration, instructional staff supervision, and organizational leadership of a school building.

SCHOOL REFORM

School reform refers to modifying schools in modest ways, such as raising standards, lengthening the school year, and establishing more stringent graduation requirements [see National Commission on Excellence in Education (1983) for examples of school reform].

SCHOOL RESTRUCTURING

School restructuring refers to substantial change in the educational process, such as site-based management, flexible schedules, exhibitions of performance for graduation, and integrated courses [see Sizer, T. (1992), *Horace's School* for an example of school restructuring].

SCHOOL TRANSFORMATION

School transformation refers to radically modifying the form and substance of education by reinterpreting teaching, learning, and knowledge. Teachers become guides. Learners become creators. Knowledge becomes a process of information literacy [see Papert, S. (1980), *Mind Storms*; Papert, S. (1993), *The Children's Machine: Rethinking school in the age of computers*; or Perelman, L. J. (1992), *School's Out* for examples of school transformation].

SYSTEMIC CHANGE

Systemic change is change that "is more complex and of wider scope, akin to redesigning a system; it alters roles, routines, and relationships within an organization" (David, 1989, p. 52). Systemic change is analogous to the transition to learning organizations implied by Peter Senge in *The Fifth Discipline* (1990), and the second-order change outlined by Larry Cuban in *The Managerial Imperative* (1988).

CHAPTER 1

How to Use This Handbook

This chapter provides basic directions on how principals and technology leaders can use this handbook to establish technology-based learning in their schools.

KEY QUESTION

What are the main parts of this handbook?

This handbook is designed as a resource book for principals and technology leaders seeking to use emerging technologies in altering learning programs. This handbook is not designed to be read in a linear, cover-to-cover fashion. It is designed so that the reader can access information in any order (see Figure 1—Handbook Process, page 8). A list of suggested readings appears at the end of each chapter.

PART I
BACKGROUND INFORMATION FOR BUILDING PRINCIPALS

This section outlines the principal's role in the changing paradigm caused by information technologies. PART I is required reading for those seeking background information supporting change in learning practices caused by emerging technologies. There are two chapters in this section. The first chapter outlines the changed paradigm of education and society; the second identifies the principal's role as an educational change leader.

PART II
TECHNOLOGY-BASED LEARNING METHODS

This section provides a model for understanding new technology-based learning methods. This model is based on the center of control for the learning process. The first chapter of this section should be read by all principals and technology leaders who want to grasp the overall pattern of the subsequent five chapters. Investigate the subsequent chapters of this section, the five technology learning methods, in any order.

PART III
IMPLEMENTING TECHNOLOGY-BASED LEARNING

This section contains two chapters. The first of these chapters, Technology Adoption Model, provides a flowchart and a checklist for principals or technology leaders to use when adopting specific technology-based learning methods. This narrative should be read as a brief planning outline for principals to begin implementation of chosen technology-based learning methods.

The second chapter, Professional Development, is an introduction to the often overlooked or underfunded aspect of technology adoption—staff development. Entire books have been devoted to this topic. However brief the treatment of staff development is in this book, effective principals and technology leaders aggressively pursue resources strategies for the development of their staff.

PART IV
RESOURCES FOR TECHNOLOGY ADOPTION
BY PRINCIPALS

The final section is a collection of resources principals can use as they develop programs and work with stakeholders on technology learning plans. Resources included in this section are: glossary, transparencies, vendors, checklists, and bibliography.

KEY QUESTION

What are the five steps to using this handbook?

STEP 1

Read Chapter 1 for background material on how to use this handbook.

STEP 2

Read Chapters 2 and 3 for material covering the change in education and society from an Industrial Age to an Information Age, and how the role of the building principal has changed.

STEP 3

Read Chapter 4 to understand how the technology-based learning model is used in this handbook.

STEP 4

Select a technology-based learning method (TLM) to investigate. If the principal and stakeholders feel a TLM has merit, go to step 5. If a TLM is unsuitable for this building or district, repeat step 4 and select another TLM for investigation.

STEP 5

Use the flowchart in Chapter 10 and other technology planning materials to implement the chosen technology-based learning method. Read Chapter 11 for a brief introduction into sound staff development practices that ensure technological integration.

Figure 1

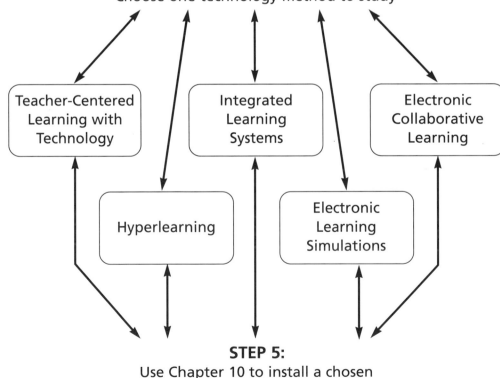

Handbook Process

STEP 1: Read Chapter 1

Introduction: How to Use This Handbook

STEP 2: Read Chapters 2 and 3

Industrial Era to Information Age;
Building Principals and Information Age Learning

STEP 3: Read Chapter 4

A Technology-Based Learning Model

STEP 4:

Choose one technology method to study

| Teacher-Centered Learning with Technology | Integrated Learning Systems | Electronic Collaborative Learning |

| Hyperlearning | Electronic Learning Simulations |

STEP 5:

Use Chapter 10 to install a chosen
technology-based learning method

FIGURE 1: Handbook Process

PART I

Background Information for Building Principals

CHAPTER 2

Industrial Era to Information Age

This chapter provides background information on how technologies are changing schools and society.

KEY QUESTION:

How are changes in the nonacademic world impacting schools?

Currently, America is in the middle of an era of educational upheaval. During this era, many assumptions and practices of schooling are being challenged. This educational change effort is fueled by a paradigm shift (Barker, 1992; Kuhn, 1962) from an Industrial Age to an Information Age (McCarthy,1991; Nadler and Hibino, 1990; Naisbitt and Aburdene, 1990; Toffler, 1990). This paradigm shift is fundamental to understanding current school change efforts.

This paradigm shift from an industrial to an information society should have urged school administrators to speed reforms of educational programs. Often it has not. Paralleling this paradigm shift from an Industrial to an Information Age are calls for fundamental educational change (Daggett, 1989; Deming, 1986; National Education Goals Panel, 1991; Perelman, 1992; Reich, 1991; U.S. Department of Labor, 1991). The world is changing "quickly, deeply and widely," but schools have been slow to recognize and react to these changes (White, 1987, p. 41).

One hope for successful school restructuring in this maelstrom of change has been emerging technologies. While there has been some debate about the role of technology in student learning, there has been widespread anticipation that electronic learning methods provide a path around current unsuccessful change efforts (Bell and Elmquist, 1992; Bruder, 1990; Cawelti, 1991; Collins, 1991; Cuban, 1992; Gibbon, 1987; Jancich, 1991; Mecklenberger, 1990; Papert, 1984; Pearlman, 1991; Perelman, 1989, 1990, and 1990a; Scheingold, 1991). Emerging technologies have provided strong links for acquainting students with the learning skills needed to survive in the Information Age (Johnston, 1985; Newhard, 1987; U. S. Congress Office of Technology Assessment, 1988; White, 1987, and 1991). At the core of these educational change efforts are emerging technologies. These emerging technologies challenge many fundamental assumptions of education.

CHAPTER 3

Building Principals and Information Age Learning

This chapter provides a brief description of the role of the building principal in an Information Age school. Also, this chapter provides a three-part framework for using emerging technologies in the learning process.

Recommended Readings for PART I, Background Information for Building Principals

Bailey, G. D., and G. L. Bailey (1994). *101 Activities for Creating Effective Technology Staff Development Programs: A book of games, stories, role playing and learning exercises for administrators.* New York: Scholastic.

Bailey, G. D., and D. Lumley (1993). *Technology Staff Development Programs: A leadership sourcebook for school administrators.* New York: Scholastic.

Barker, J. A. (1992). *Future Edge: Discovering the new paradigms of success.* New York: William Morrow.

Cetron, M., and M. Gayle (1991). *Educational Renaissance: Our schools at the turn of the 21st century.* New York: St. Martin's Press.

Fullan, M. G., and S. Stiegelbauer (1991). *The New Meaning of Educational Change.* New York: Teachers College Press.

Gardner, H. (1985). *Frames of Mind: The theory of multiple intelligences.* New York: Basic Books.

McLuhan, M. (1962). *The Gutenberg Galaxy: The making of typographic man.* Toronto: University of Toronto Press.

Mecklenberger, J. A. (1990). The New Revolution. Special reprint from *Business Week,* No. 3191, 22–26.

Nadler, G., and S. Hibino (1990). *Breakthrough Thinking: Why we must change the way we solve problems, and the seven principles to achieve this.* Rocklin, CA: Prima Publishing.

Papert, S. (1980). *Mindstorms: Children, computers, and powerful ideas.* New York: Basic Books.

————. (1984). New Theories for New Learning. *School Psychology Review, 13*(4), 422–428.

Perelman, L. J. (1992). *School's Out: Hyperlearning, the new technology, and the end of education.* New York: William Morrow.

Reich, R. B. (1991). *The Work of Nations: Preparing ourselves for 21st century capitalism.* New York: Alfred A. Knopf.

Scheingold, K., and M. S. Tucker (eds.) (1990). *Restructuring for Learning With Technology.* New York: Center for Technology in Education and the National Center on Education and the Economy.

Toffler, A. (1990). *Power Shift: Knowledge, wealth and violence at the edge of the 21st century.* New York: Bantam Books.

U. S. Congress, Office of Technology Assessment (1988). *Power On! New tools for teaching and learning.* Washington, DC: U. S. Government Printing Office.

U. S. Department of Labor: Secretary's Commission on Achieving Necessary Skills (1991). *What Work Requires of Schools: A SCANS report on America 2000*. Washington, DC: U. S. Government Printing Office.

White, M. A. (ed.) (1983). *The Future of Electronic Learning*. Hillsdale, NJ: Lawrence Erlbaum Associates.

————. (ed.) (1987). *What Curriculum for the Information Age*? Hillsdale, NJ: Lawrence Erlbaum Associates.

7

PART II

Technology-Based Learning Methods

CHAPTER 4

A Technology-Based Learning Model

This chapter provides a model for building principals and technology leaders to conceptualize new learning methods using emerging technologies. Five technology-based learning methods are provided.

KEY QUESTION

Is there a model to help conceptualize learning in the Information Age?

Principals need models to conceptualize emerging educational technologies within the overall framework of school change. This principal's handbook provides a model based on five technology-based learning methods; each method is built on the concept of **learner control**. This model focuses on learning and technology's role in the learning process. This does not relegate technology to the background of instruction, but centralizes technology in the learning process.

LEARNER CONTROL

The learner and the center of learning control are the essential features of this model. As part of the paradigm shift from Industrial Age to Information Age schooling, this model investigates education not from an instructional, teacher, front-of-the-classroom perspective but from a learner, student, back-of-the-classroom perspective.

The five technology-based learning methods outlined by this model inevitably become complicated since each one is bound up with every other. One method cannot be described without calling all other methods into consideration. **However, it is convenient at this time to separate this model into five methods, as though they were unrelated.**[1]

Learner control is a critical component of the educational process. Traditional instructional practice has the teacher as the sole focus of learning. Teachers instruct as a sage-on-the-stage. As the center for learner control changes from the sole teacher to many centers of learning, the role of the teacher changes to that of an aide, coach, motivator, facilitator, questioner, or guide-on-the-side. As teachers' roles change, principals change from examining the instructional process to examining the learning process. The five methods that will be outlined in this model are based on a change in the control of the learning process brought about by emerging technologies.

School change surrounds the core of technology-based learning methods. The core efforts of technology-based learning methods are grouped in overlapping circles (see Figure 2—Technology-Based Learning Methods). Each circle represents a central learning methodology using emerging technologies. The methods are: teacher-centered learning with technology, integrated learning systems, electronic collaborative learning, hyperlearning, and electronic learning simulations.

---

[1] It must be remembered that such a separation is an oversimplification.

Figure 2

Technology-Based Learning Methods

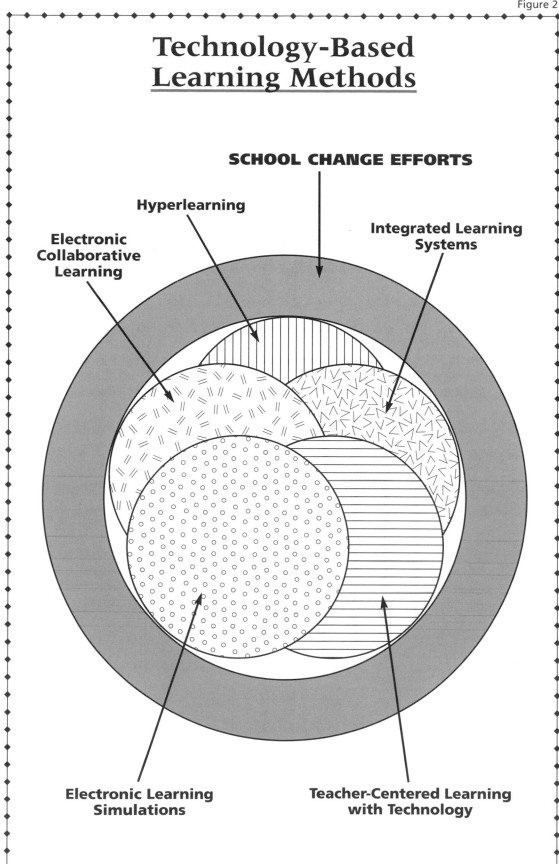

FIGURE 2: *Technology-Based Learning Methods*   23

- ◆ **TEACHER-CENTERED LEARNING WITH TECHNOLOGY.**
  Teacher-centered learning uses electronic technologies to provide
  instruction in traditional linear fashion: lecture, recitation, directed
  questioning. **The teacher sets the pace of instruction and the
  subject matter.**

- ◆ **INTEGRATED LEARNING SYSTEMS**. Integrated learning
  systems (ILSs) allow for accomplishment of specific learning
  outcomes through the use of computer technologies. **The
  machine, with a measure of teacher input, through highly
  structured, programmed administrative software, sets the
  pace of instruction and the subject matter.**

- ◆ **ELECTRONIC COLLABORATIVE LEARNING.** Electronic
  collaborative learning uses emerging technologies for collaboration
  and cooperation among learners who may be separated by time or
  distance. **The collaborative team sets the pace and direction
  of learning.**

- ◆ **HYPERLEARNING**. Hyperlearning (Perelman, 1992) is an
  organizing principle recognizing the multidimensional fabric of
  knowledge linked with all its intellectual antecedents.
  Hyperlearning allows learners to follow preferences and control
  their own learning (Bevilacqua, 1989). **The learner sets the
  pace, order, and depth of instruction and subject matter**.

- ◆ **ELECTRONIC LEARNING SIMULATIONS**. Electronic learning
  simulations create environments for learning through electronic
  technologies. With this method students explore electronically
  created worlds. **The electronic simulation, with a strong
  measure of learner input, sets the pace of instruction and
  the subject matter.**

KEY QUESTION

What are the features of each technology-based learning method?

This five-part technology learning model has several features that need to be rec-
ognized at the outset.

- ◆ There is no hierarchical order to the learning methods. Principals
  can adopt or implement any learning method(s) in any order that
  suits their goals.

◆ There is much overlap of the learning methods. Strategies within each learning method cause these methods to have much in common. For example, an article in *Electronic Learning* announced interactive video, teacher presentation tools, electronic mail, and a national bulletin board all under the umbrella of an integrated learning system (Hill, 1993).

◆ These are learning methods for all learners and subject matters. These learning methods can be used with a wide range of talents and subjects. A learning method is not exclusively designed for a specific category of learner. Principals and planning teams should choose learning models to match the needs of particular students, subject material, levels of expertise, or learning goals.

◆ Learning, particularly in the latter methods, is an active process. Students are not recipients of instruction but are active participants in choosing the depth and range of their own learning.

KEY QUESTION

What were the criteria for the selection of each of these technology-based learning methods?

Why were these technology-based learning methods chosen as examples? The selection criteria for each of these major methods of technology-based learning were: 1) current use in education or industry; 2) use of technology to empower major learning strategies; and 3) within the domain of school change and emerging electronic learning technologies. The learning methods matrix on the following page (Figure 3—Learning Methods Matrix) provides an example of these major methods with a delineation of the center of control, major strategies within each method, and examples from business and industry. Learning-centered methods implement the five competencies outlined by the SCANS (1991) report.

The technology-based learning model provides principals with a useful conceptual tool to evaluate the role of technology in the educational process.

However, there are several other programs that provide educational change models that may occur simultaneously with the technology-based learning model and help to bring about overall restructuring or transformation of schools. Some of these are: the six-step plan of America 2000 (McREL, 1990), overhaul of schooling infrastructure (Hodgkinson, 1991), alternative methods for evaluation of student progress (Sizer, 1992; Center for Children and Technology, Bank Street College, 1990), and alternative school scheduling practices (Sizer, 1992). English and Hill (1990) provided a useful outline of the many differences between current educational practices and restructured schools.

Figure 3

Learning Methods Matrix

LEARNING METHOD	CENTER OF CONTROL	WORLD OF WORK EXAMPLE	STRATEGIES
Teacher-centered learning with technology	Teacher: The teacher directs the pace and sequence.	Training sessions, specific skill development	Multimedia presentation, videotape, distance instruction
Integrated learning systems	Machine: A computer network and its software directs the learning.	Teaching machines	Distributed ILS, lab-centered ILS
Electronic collaborative learning	Teams/partners: The team negotiates, goals, pacing, and sequence of learning.	Developmental teams, joint research efforts, learning teams	Local area networks, wide area networks, cooperative ventures
Hyperlearning	Learner: The learner is in charge of pace and sequence of learning.	Research, market analysis, engineering design	Hypertext development, hypermedia development, multimedia development, network searching
Electronic learning simulations	Machine and learner: Learning is in joint control.	Flight simulators, disaster control simulations, war games	Virtual reality electronic simulations

26

FIGURE 3: Learning Methods Matrix

KEY QUESTION

What are the critical elements of each TLM?

ELEMENTS OF THE LEARNING METHOD

To help principals navigate each technology-based learning method, there are nine elements that address specific issues important to building principals. Each of these elements is identified by an icon. Below are the nine elements and the corresponding icon used in each learning method. They are in the order in which they appear within each learning method.

Element #1
OVERVIEW

The overview section of each method contains a one-sentence concept of the methodology, the center of learning control, and a discussion about how this method can be used in the classroom.

Element #2
PAYOFFS

The payoffs section of each method lists advantages principals can anticipate from adopting a technology-based learning method.

Element #3
STRATEGIES

The strategies section of each method outlines classroom strategies using emerging technologies that support a technology-based learning method.

Element #4

STAFF

The staff section sets out benefits and difficulties of the learning method for staff members. This section concludes with a discussion of what characteristics principals should expect from staff members using a technology-based learning method.

Element #5

STUDENTS

The students section sets out benefits and difficulties of the learning method for students. This section concludes with a discussion of what characteristics principals should expect from students using a technology-based learning method.

Element #6

FACILITIES

The facilities section of each method lists possible construction or remodeling concerns principals will need to address when adopting a technology-based learning method.

Element #7

BUDGET

The budget section of each method highlights financial considerations principals must examine when adopting a technology-based learning method.

Element #8

TIPS-TRICKS-TRAPS

This section provides useful techniques for principals considering implementation of a technology-based learning method along with some pitfalls to be avoided for successful implementation.

Element #9
<u>EXAMPLES</u>

As a final element in each technology-based learning method, a few examples of actual classroom use of technology have been included. These examples were selected from hundreds of possibilities. Often the examples chosen covered more than one technology-based learning method. The illustrations were chosen to be exemplary, not comprehensive. Many more examples can be found in *Electronic Learning*, *The Computing Teacher*, and Betty Collis's *Computers, Curriculum and Whole-Class Instruction*.

SUMMARY

The core section of this handbook is based on centers of learning. Five technology-based learning methods surrounding centers of learning and using emerging technology are examined: teacher-centered learning with technology (teacher), integrated learning systems (machine), electronic collaborative learning (learning team), hyperlearning (individual learner), and electronic learning simulations (machine and learner together). Each of these learning methods is clarified using nine elements: overview, payoffs, strategies, staff, students, facilities, budget, tips-tricks-traps, and examples.

Recommended Readings for Chapter 4:
A Technology-Based Learning Model

Bevilacqua, A. F. (1989). *Hypertext: Behind the hype*. ERIC Document Reproduction Service, No. ED 308 882.

Business Week (1992). Reinventing America: Meeting the new challenges of a global economy. Special issue *Business Week,* No. 3191.

English, F. W., and J. C. Hill (1990). *Restructuring: The principal and curriculum change*. Reston, VA: National Association of Secondary School Principals.

Perelman, L. J. (1992). *School's Out: Hyperlearning, the new technology, and the end of education*. New York: William Morrow.

U.S. Department of Labor, Secretary's Commission on Achieving Necessary Skills (1991). *What Work Requires of Schools: A SCANS report on America 2000*. Washington, DC: U. S. Government Printing Office.

CHAPTER 5

Teacher-Centered Learning with Technology

Teacher-centered learning with technology is a reform methodology in which classroom instructors maintain their traditional role but use emerging technologies as enhancements of instruction.

KEY QUESTION

How do schools use technology to improve learning?

OVERVIEW

CONCEPT

Teacher-centered learning with technology uses technological enhancements to continue traditional instructional strategies.

CENTER OF LEARNING CONTROL

The teacher using emerging technology is the center of learning control.

DISCUSSION

In teacher-centered learning with technology, education is led by instructors who enhance delivery of subject matter using technology. Traditional strategies of lecture, dialogue, guided questions, and student evaluation continue unabated. However, new techniques of multimedia presentation, video display, distance teaching, etc. are added dimensions to previous instructional strategies. In teacher-centered instruction, emerging technologies are tools of the instructional process. These technologies alter the basic pattern of instruction very little. Measurable student outcomes appear to be a strong feature of teacher-centered learning with technology.

Teacher-centered learning with technology, in the hands of skilled instructors, can be used in a variety of ways to enhance learning: drill and practice for review of basic skills, interaction with the class, individualization of lessons, motivation for learning, accessing different intelligences, instructional delivery across town or across the nation, and so on. Learning objectives are maintained by the instructor. New ways of presentation and reinforcement are provided by teachers through technology.

PAYOFFS

Teacher-centered learning with technology has many of the same advantages as teacher-centered learning prior to the advent of electronic instructional technology. Among the advantages of teacher-led instruction are:

- ◆ Basic skill acquisition

- ◆ Sequential introduction of new material

- ◆ Measurable objectives and accomplishments

Added to this list of advantages with teacher-centered instruction using technology are:

- ◆ Renewed teacher enthusiasm

- ◆ Increased student motivation

- ◆ Better techniques for classroom demonstration

- ◆ Increased accuracy in reporting results from student experiments

- ◆ Greater visual portrayal of complex subjects

- ◆ Increased sharing of scarce instructional resources through distance learning

- ◆ Improved classroom lessons using multimedia: sound, graphics, video, and animation

STRATEGIES

Principals can observe several variations of teacher-centered learning with technology. These variations follow.

TEACHER PRESENTATION WITH TECHNOLOGY

Often in this strategy, multimedia presentation by teachers is analogous with lecture as a means of delivery. The teacher, at the front of the class, presents lessons using sound, graphics, animation, pictures, and video employing equipment controlled by a computer. In addition to a computer, equipment used in this strategy may include

CHAPTER 5: Teacher-Centered Learning with Technology 33

speakers, LCD panels, large monitors, videotape recorders, overhead projectors, and laser disc machines (D'Ignazio, 1990a). Daiute (1992) makes an effective argument for using multimedia to teach basic reading and writing skills. This strategy views technology as a tool to enhance traditional educational programs, not a factor to radically alter the educational process.

INDIVIDUAL STUDENT ASSIGNMENTS

Teachers direct students to complete homework assignments using electronic technologies. This may include computers and specific software programs for word processing (e.g., English), spreadsheet (e.g., accounting), database (e.g., social studies), or computer-aided drawing (e.g., industrial arts). Often these assignments need little sophisticated equipment. Math assignments can be completed using a handheld, "talking" calculator. Writing assignments can be completed with a credit card–size spell checker.

MICRO-BASED LABORATORIES

Using appropriate scientific apparatuses and software, computers measure, record, graph, and analyze a variety of physical properties such as temperature, light, pH, pressure, and electrical and mechanical properties (Morse, 1991).

COMPUTER-ASSISTED INSTRUCTION (CAI)

In this strategy a single stand-alone computer can be used to provide or enhance instruction for students in a specific skill. It differs from an ILS in the size of the management system, number of machines involved, and scope of material covered.

TEACHER-CENTERED LEARNING OVER DISTANCE

Many schools have found that instructional television delivered by broadcast, cable, or satellite has been an effective strategy to share scarce resources in several classrooms. Distance learning is the use of telecommunications equipment such as telephone, television fiber optics, cable broadcast, and satellites to send instructional programming to learners (Bruder, 1991). Teacher-centered learning at a distance often uses television with students and teachers at different locations involved in two-way educational interaction. This strategy has been particularly valuable in isolated areas where classroom populations are small. The costs and talents of specialized teachers (e.g., foreign language and advanced science) can be shared among several school districts. Some states, Kentucky and Kansas for example, have invested heavily in distance television instruction.[1]

Many unresolved issues deter the effective use of a distance-learning strategy.

---

[1] See Transparency TCL 1 for an example of a distance learning network in southwest Kansas.

Among these issues are teacher certification, responsibility for the educational programming, and questions of teacher contracts and compensation. Isabelle Bruder (1989) outlined several concerns that must be addressed by principals investigating distance-learning strategies.

ONE-WAY PROGRAM DELIVERY

Many schools have opted to receive information in the classroom from one-way, noninteractive television. In this strategy students are passive recipients of instruction, often current events or news programming. This information is delivered in much the same format as television at home. It is estimated that one-third of U.S. teenagers view current events programming provided at no charge to the school. Two popular sources of educational television programming have been Corporation for Public Broadcasting and National Geographic.

STAFF

Teachers find the ability to present complex material with electronic enhancements exhilarating. They can visually present difficult concepts, make attractive visuals, and realistically recreate events difficult to observe because of time, distance, danger, or rarity. Apple Computer, Inc., describes teacher presentation stations as one of the main delivery tools for multimedia (Apple Computer, Inc., 1990).

However, unless teachers have adequate training using these materials, the process can be very frustrating and confusing. Teacher-centered instruction with technology is highly dependent upon teachers' attitudes toward this means of instructing children. Teachers must be comfortable with electronic devices they are given to enhance instruction. Developing instructional competence and confidence with emerging technological equipment is one of the crucial roles of principals integrating technology in their schools. Staff development for teachers is an often overlooked or underfunded aspect of technology integration in schools. In fulfilling their leadership role, principals must seek, support, and cultivate educators who are able to:

- ◆ Evaluate and use software in different educational settings

- ◆ Describe the purposes and major features of application software

- ◆ Identify sources for computer education materials in all subject areas

- ◆ Relate learning theory and principles of child development to the creation of a computer learning environment

- ◆ Discuss major issues in computer education

- Apply their knowledge of curriculum development to develop supplemental materials to use with computer software

- Develop a few simple programs or products using technology

- Interpret research findings, theory, and literature in the field

- Discuss characteristic strengths and weaknesses of different programming languages (Adams and Hamm, 1987)[2]

What should principals look for when observing staff members using teacher-centered learning technology methods?

- Teachers taking risks in lesson preparation with technology.

- Teachers leading attractive, exciting activities with technology.

- Teachers addressing a variety of student needs and learning styles with technology.

- Teachers at different levels of multimedia instructional expertise: authoring, using, and experimenting.

STUDENTS

Depending upon the emerging technology used by the instructor, students benefit from many different instructional elements. Often these demonstration technologies allow material to be placed in a visual framework. Teacher demonstrations of mathematical solutions or scientific experiments are one example using a computer and projection device. Video technology allows students to see contemporary versions of famous stories performed by classical actors. Multimedia technologies allow for comparative versions of the same learning material. Distance learning technologies allow students in one location to follow instruction led by an instructor in another. This technology allows schools separated by distance to share the benefits of teacher specialization and expertise.

Students benefit from technology by having time-consuming, repetitive examples

---

[2] The International Society for Technology in Education (ISTE) submitted to the National Council of Accreditation Education (NCATE) its recommendations for a set of national accreditation standards for education technology. These make a suitable "starting point" for principals seeking to determine the qualities needed by their computer-using instructional staff members.

presented numerous ways using interesting graphics and other multisensory techniques. Examples of this strategy are seen in the emphasis on calculators and graphing calculators in the new math standards (Bruder, Buchsbaum, Hill, and Orlando, 1992). Demonstrations also allow simulated practice with situations that are too dangerous or rare to practice in real life.

What should principals look for when observing students using teacher-centered learning technology methods?

- ◆ Students show increased enthusiasm for classroom lessons.

- ◆ Students demonstrate a deeper understanding of complex material.

- ◆ Students demonstrate a faster comprehension of complex material.

- ◆ Students demonstrate greater connection between classroom learning and real-world examples.

- ◆ Students demonstrate learning that reflects their unique intelligence.

- ◆ Students enroll in classes offered and taught by instructors in different locations.

FACILITIES

Teacher-centered instruction using emerging technology may require little facility revision. Most electronic instruction can proceed with no modification to traditional classrooms. Lighting, electrical power, and projection areas are basic considerations. These need to be addressed in construction or remodeling projects. Many classrooms are sufficient with little modification.

Much of the emerging technology equipment used in the teacher-centered mode of instruction can be placed on carts and moved around school buildings that meet guidelines for handicapped accessibility. Equipment can be stored in central locations and checked out to teachers as needed. If connection to a network is needed, additional wiring will be required.

However, if distance learning via television is chosen as a strategy, facility requirements can be extensive. The Minnesota Department of Education found planning and construction for television demonstration stations cost between $131,400 and $1,082,805. Their annualized operating costs averaged $56,435 (Morehouse, Hoaglund, and Schmidt, 1987). Conversely, thousands of dollars of video equipment has been placed in classrooms around the nation at no cost to school districts by Whittle Communications (Rist, 1991).

BUDGET

Budgeting for teacher instructional centers is extremely flexible. Expenditures are tailored to subject matter. Some subjects may require a great deal of expense for software; others may not.

Deborah Branscum (1992) suggested five strategies to save money when purchasing technology hardware and software.

SHAREWARE-FREEWARE

User groups and others belonging to on-line systems find surprisingly good software available over modems or for purchase through user groups at reasonable prices.

LOW-COST COMMERCIAL SOFTWARE

Unless there is a specific need for powerful drawing, spreadsheet, or word processing programs, many low-cost, reasonably featured packages are available in the $50–$200 range.

INTEGRATED PACKAGES

While integrated packages usually cost more than low-end, stand-alone software, they offer good value for the money. Most integrated packages include word processing, database, spreadsheet, and drawing modules.

USED HARDWARE

Good used equipment can be purchased through local classified ads, computer brokers, or direct-mail companies. However, care and technical expertise may be required to ensure that such equipment is in good condition and meets the software requirements for memory and processing speed.

PENNY-PINCHERS

Many companies offer program upgrades at reasonable prices. There are many direct mail catalogs that offer significant savings in price.

Branscum addressed her money-saving techniques toward the purchase of computer equipment. Principals working on a tight budget should not overlook local electronic stores for many of their technology purchases.[3]

Another tactic principals may wish to pursue is leasing equipment. This tactic may

---

[3] See Transparency TCL 2 for a graphical review of money-saving techniques.

provide a way to acquire expensive equipment and at the same time avoid having the school saddled with expensive equipment that rapidly becomes obsolete. Apple and IBM both provide leasing or lease purchase options for schools.

TIPS-TRICKS-TRAPS

TIPS

TIP #1
If technology resources are going to be shared by teachers from room to room, make sure the cart they are to be carried on is sturdy, has large wheels for rolling over obstructions, and is equipped to "plug and play." The equipment must need only one plug-in and one switch to turn everything on. Also, be sure the cart is checked out as a unit. Individual devices and cables must remain with the cart and not be scavenged for other uses. Assign one individual responsibility for maintaining and scheduling the equipment.

TIP #2
"Grantsmanship" is an effective strategy for getting resources for the classroom. Often school districts, to encourage innovative practices in the classroom, have grant programs. Before authorizing these grants, principals should check to make sure they match the curriculum goals of the school.

TIP #3
Principals can encourage teachers to form partnerships with local businesses to provide technology learning experiences for students. Some corporations provide mini-grants.

TIP #4
Some teachers are reluctant to use technology in their classrooms because technology means more work for them. To win these reluctant users over, principals should provide ways for technology to ease the workload of classroom teachers. Two ways to do this may be to provide a computer for each teacher and electronic mail for communication.

TIP #5
Teachers must model technology use for their students. Students must see the teachers using emerging technologies for both instruction and management. Teachers who preach technology but do not practice it send conflicting messages to students. Staff development for teachers is absolutely essential. This staff development must be at two levels: skills level and conceptual level. Principals may want to investigate sources specific to staff development, such as Bailey and Lumley (1994).

TIP #6

Many strategies and tactics for acquiring funds to initiate and institute technology-based learning methods can be gleaned from the work of others. David Bauer (1993) has published a series of monographs that outline effective ways of developing the financial resources necessary to institutionalize a technology-based learning method.

TRICKS

TRICK #1

When students use technology for school board demonstrations, Parent's Night, or community programs, they are building support for the school technology program. Make sure these audiences understand how this technology is used every day in the business world and how the students are gaining skills they will use after they complete their formal education.

TRICK #2

Finding ways to use equipment as it becomes outdated is an ongoing strategy to expand the use of technology in schools. Much of this equipment can start students on new ways of communication using multimedia projects. Fred D'Ignazio (1989a, 1989b, 1990e, 1991c) designed programs around scavenged equipment for multimedia.

TRICK #3

Planned abandonment is a necessary part of integrating technology into the regular classroom. Principals must plan for abandoning outdated instructional practices and equipment. Tradition or community standards often hinder efforts to eliminate some outdated programs and practices. Abandonment of tried and traditional practices is often controversial. What is the role, for example, of the county spelling bee in a curriculum full of spell checkers?

TRAPS

TRAP #1

Technology equipment used only for remediation or reward is often unconnected to the curriculum. This technology does not become part of the curriculum but serves as an add-on to the regular program. Parents who see kids playing games may be observing technology unconnected to the curriculum. Principals must ensure that technologies are used to support curricular purposes.

TRAP #2

Teachers are often given or request technology for their classroom with little or no training in its effective instructional use. For effective use of technology in classrooms, teachers must have the skills to run the equipment, an understanding of how the equipment enhances student learning, and the opportunity to practice both. These technology skills can materialize only through effective, ongoing, technology staff development activities.

EXAMPLES

HANDS-ON MATH AND SCIENCE

In an Alabama school science class a variety of sensors and probes are connected to Macintosh computers. This effectively changes the computers into oscilloscopes, temperature probes, pressure sensors, or light meters. Students use this equipment to make science come alive through hands-on activities. They take control of physics and chemistry experiments and, given the greater accuracy of the computer sensors, the students are able to develop projects that come much closer to theoretical values than would be possible with traditional methods (McCarthy, 1992).

WRITING TO LEARN

A class of low-achieving students was lent a roomful of IBM PC Jrs. to help them learn how to write effectively. Suddenly, the classroom was changed from a room of low achievers to one of high-achieving students writing more complex and meaningful sentences. The instructor observed a major shift in student attitudes about writing. Some of the previously low-achieving students signed up to take the Advanced Placement English class (Hill, 1992c).

BEYOND DRILL AND PRACTICE IN A ONE-COMPUTER CLASSROOM

Even with minimal equipment, enthusiastic instructors can develop effective learning activities that accomplish goals established by the teacher. One example was a second-grade classroom with only one computer. By rotating the use of the computer, 22 students wrote letters of at least five sentences. In a subsequent assignment, the teacher used this one computer to have the students write cooperative geography reports. The first software package used in this classroom was *Magic Slate*. Soon the students advanced to *Children's Writing and Publishing Center*. "When you do drills and practice at the computer, the computer is in charge of learning. When you word process, the person at the keyboard is truly the master of his or her own learning." (Weisberg, 1992).

GAINING FLUENCY

The staff of a special-needs classroom wanted to help their students access a modern language curriculum. They started by using a Canon Ion still video camera. After returning to school from a field trip to a local French grocery store, the pictures were viewed as a springboard for discussing the experience. One of the instructors used a software package to create an on-screen supermarket. These special-need students stocked the on-screen shelves using the appropriate foreign language labels (Hughes, 1992).

BLACKBOARD DISK JOCKEYS

Student age or grade level has little to do with the effectiveness of technology to enhance teacher-centered learning. With five computers and one CD-ROM, a kindergarten teacher used technology to study language arts and science. The teacher was particularly pleased that the technology addressed a variety of student learning styles: visual, auditory, and tactile (Hill, 1993a).

THE STUDENT MAESTRO

At a variety of schools, from inner-city to rural, music educators are using technology to change student perceptions about music. Included in the technologies being used to bring about this change have been MTV, CD-ROMS, and keyboards. Using Yamaha's *Music in Education* series, students have listened to, played, and learned various aspects of music composition. In one school an innovative teacher asked students to choose a song from their favorite musical group. Using *HyperCard* stacks and Voyager's *CD Audio Toolkit,* students annotated the musical compositions with text and graphics (Solomon, 1993).

LIGHTS, ACTION, MATH

Three new programs were used to lead instruction for the integration of the National Council of Teachers of Mathematics's math standards. The first of the three programs is *Fundamental Math.* This series of videotapes contains 30 specific math concepts. The second is Tom Snyder's *The Graph Club,* which integrates a graphing tool, a manipulative software environment, and a comprehensive curriculum guide. The third is *Hands-On Math,* a simulation of 17 lessons using math manipulatives such as rods, counters, and a number balance (Lindroth, 1994).

THE HIGH SCHOOL OFFICE

This office practice classroom of the future looks just like the office of a modern corporation. It contains up-to-date equipment, including computers, fax machines, copy machines, and telephones. Students are involved in typical office activities, and there is a general feeling of purpose and attention to business. The difference is, this office is in a school, and these students are using technology to master modern business skills (Apple Computer Inc., 1991).

VIDEO NETWORK TO CONNECT STUDENTS IN SEVEN SCHOOLS

Space-age technology has given students in small rural communities more class choices and opportunities for learning. Seven schools in a rural area joined together to create a fiber-optic network that allows students and teachers to communicate between schools. Students can now enroll in courses that their small schools cannot afford to provide. Each school is able to capitalize on the strengths of its teaching staff, and all students benefit (Bittinger, 1991, June 11).

TECHNOLOGY IN SPECIAL EDUCATION

In a Michigan high school, students with special needs regularly visit a room with three computers where they catch up with assignments established in traditional classrooms. Some of the students have learning disabilities, some have emotional impairments, and others have attention deficit disorders. All, however, were behind in traditional course work. The use of these computers helps them catch up with their assignments because they can write faster, they can work at their own pace, and the computers hold their interest (Holzberg, 1994).

Recommended Readings for Chapter 5:
Teacher-Centered Learning with Technology

Bailey, G. D., and D. Lumley (1994). *Technology Staff Development Programs: A leadership sourcebook for administrators.* New York: Scholastic.

Bauer, D. G. (1994). *The Principal's Guide to Grant Success.* New York: Scholastic.

Bruder, I., H. Buchsbaum, M. Hill, and L. C. Orland (1992). School Reform: Why you need technology to get there. *Electronic Learning, 11*(8), 22–28.

Buerry, L., K. Haslan, and N. Legters (1990). Images of Potential: From vision to reality. Special reprint from *Business Week, No. 3191,* 50–53.

Dede, C. (1987). Empowering Environments, Hypermedia and Microworlds. *The Computing Teacher, 15*(3), 20–24.

D'Ignazio, F. (1989). Getting Started with Multimedia: 16 classroom strategies. *The Computing Teacher, 16*(3), 17–19.

Lumley, D., and G. D. Bailey (1993). *Planning for Technology: A guidebook for school administrators.* New York: Scholastic.

Whisler, J. S. (1988). Distance Learning Technologies: An aid to restructuring schools? In Mid-Continent Regional Educational Laboratory. *Noteworthy,* 28–41. Washington, DC: U. S. Government Printing Office.

CHAPTER 6

Integrated Learning Systems

*Integrated learning systems (ILSs)
are a restructuring methodology in
which computer networks and
management systems provide a
substantial portion of basic
skills instruction.*

> *The real problem is not whether machines think,*
> *but whether men do.*
>
> B. F. Skinner

KEY  QUESTION

How can schools using technology help students in reading, writing, and math?

OVERVIEW

CONCEPT

Students using an integrated learning system (ILS) accomplish specific learning outcomes using computer technologies; systematic monitoring; and incremental, behavioral, computer-driven teaching.

CENTER OF LEARNING CONTROL

The computer network, along with its administrative software, controls the learning process.

DISCUSSION

Integrated learning systems are perhaps the largest single comprehensive use of the emerging technologies in the United States. A recent estimate placed the number of schools that own an ILS at 7,947 (*Electronic Learning*, 1992a). Currently, the United States invests nearly half a billion dollars annually in ILSs (Butzin, 1992).

An ILS consists of networked hardware that uses complex management systems to provide individualized basic skills instruction (*Electronic Learning*, 1992). The traditional delivery of instruction through the use of an ILS is a networked facility sharing software between a large number of computers and a file server. The file server directs and monitors the flow of information to and from the other computers (Lumley & Bailey, 1990). Integrated learning systems dovetail with outcomes-based methods. They provide teachers with opportunities for reteaching and establishing mastery levels (Mageau, 1992). Often, an ILS has been positioned more to provide supplemental and remedial instruction than mainstream instruction.

ILS software connects computer devices to accomplish the following instructional tasks:

- ◆ Assessment and diagnosis of student skills

- ◆ Delivery of instruction

- ◆ Continuous monitoring of student performance with automatic instructional adjustment

- ◆ Generation of student and class performance data (Maddux and Willis, 1992)

PAYOFFS

Achievement outcomes for students using an ILS have been a source of controversy. ILSs were, in large measure, established to produce and document measurable gains in basic skills. A number of critics have attacked ILSs, noting that they have failed to support higher-order thinking skills (Sherry, 1990b; Trotter, 1990b). Becker (1992) challenged that ILSs should not be used as the sole component of effective instruction. Still, some specific benefits of ILSs have been documented by student outcomes research.

- ◆ Students are excited about working on computers (Trotter, 1990b; Sherry, 1990b).

- ◆ Parents and administrators appreciate printed reports on student's progress (Trotter, 1990b).

- ◆ Individualized instruction matches the curriculum (Trotter, 1990b; Sherry, 1990b).

- ◆ Color graphics are now available (Trotter, 1990b).

STRATEGIES

Currently there are two instructional strategies using an ILS: laboratory placement and distributed placement.

LABORATORY PLACEMENT

The first, and more common, placement of an ILS is in a laboratory. Students are sent or escorted to work in the ILS lab. The labs are usually supervised by monitors familiar with the equipment and software but lacking formal teacher training. Teachers, through the management system, establish lessons, mastery levels, and reporting schedules. They often do not accompany their students to the lab to supervise their work. This delivery strategy focuses on ILSs as a supplement to mainstream classroom instruction. There is a high correlation with traditional textbooks in an ILS lab placement.

DISTRIBUTED PLACEMENT

In the second delivery model, ILS networks are distributed throughout the building in individual classrooms. Teachers manage the same functions as with a lab-oriented ILS, but in this case small groups of students can complete the lessons at workstations in the classroom. Distributed ILS networks become an integral part of classroom instruction in this model, not a supplemental or pull-out remedial program. Teachers personally supervise student progress. Instructors maintain a subjective grasp on student learning patterns.

STAFF

Staff considerations for an ILS methodology are dependent on the type of placement established for the equipment. If a laboratory placement for an ILS program is chosen, a lab supervisor needs to be hired and trained. The lab supervisor does not need to be a fully certified teacher but does need to be familiar with the administrative program of the ILS. The lab supervisor also needs to understand the art of teaching to ensure that the learning goals of teachers are being addressed by the programming received through an ILS.

If a distributed ILS is chosen, all teachers involved with the ILS need training in the administrative program. The teachers must be able to create assignments and see to it that the goals established for students are being met. And classroom instructors must also be able to generate meaningful assessment reports on a timely basis.

In some ways, hiring a lab monitor to address the teachers' ILS needs is easier than training all teachers in managing the intricacies of the management system. And although hiring a supervisor is more expensive, principals can have greater confidence for successful supervision of the ILS system knowing that it is one person's sole responsibility. The cheaper alternative, distributed networks, puts the responsibility on classroom teachers and requires high levels of training, motivation, and supervision.

What should principals look for in staff members using integrated learning systems?

- ◆ Classroom curriculum goals incorporated into ILS instruction.

- ◆ Use of reporting and management capabilities of the ILS.

- ◆ Regular monitoring of student progress.

- ◆ Regular use of the ILS system to match student achievement to curriculum objectives.

- ◆ Effective communication between a lab monitor and instructional staff.

STUDENTS

Specific learning goals are established in incremental, behavioral steps. Students meet these goals through one of two ILS placements: a lab placement or distributed placement. In the former, students leave their regular classroom for the ILS lab, where they receive instruction via the equipment. In the latter, students remain in their regular classroom, receiving programmed instruction under the tutelage of the regular classroom teacher. Students need little training to use an ILS.

What should principals look for in students using integrated learning systems?

- ◆ Self-paced learning.

- ◆ Specific, documented achievement outcomes.

- ◆ ILS as an integral part of classroom instruction.

- ◆ Subject mastery for all students at different times.

FACILITIES

A lab arrangement for an ILS requires a specialized room large enough to hold 20 to 25 students, an instructor's station, the associated server, and printers to accompany ILS programs. Several factors must be addressed in design of the ILS lab:[1]

- Lighting

- Furniture

- Wiring

- Security

- Storage for software, paper, and supplies

- Telephone connection for modem and technical communications with vendor

SPECIALIZED MATERIALS FOR ILS INCLUDE:

- Many computers

- Dedicated server

- Mass storage devices

- Printers

- Network wiring and devices

- Specialized administrative software

- Specialized subject software

BUDGET

Depending on the courseware purchased with the installation, one recent estimate established the cost of a 25-station student ILS lab at $50,000 to $125,000 (Sherry, 1992b). Additional costs include:

- Software licensing, update, or support fees ($100 to $45,000 yearly)

- Staff training if not included in basic vendor's pricing

- Dlectrical wiring charges

- Developing available space for an ILS lab (Sherry, 1992b)

A different analysis set the cost of an ILS lab at $3,000 per workstation and $50 to $750 per station for software enhancements, updates, and upgrades (Finkel, 1992).

---

[1] See Transparency ILS 1 for a facilities checklist when considering the purchase of an ILS.

Administrative risks are proportional to anticipated expenses. Prudent principals, when shopping for expensive integrated learning systems, should consider many factors before investing in such a major capital expenditure.

- ◆ Define the need.

- ◆ Audit the present curriculum.

- ◆ Consider alternatives.

- ◆ Involve all significant stakeholders: administrators, teachers, students, and parents.

- ◆ Ensure a strong correlation between ILS courseware and curriculum.

- ◆ Plan for adequate money and personnel resources to support the ILS system.

- ◆ Look for hidden costs.

- ◆ Start with a pilot project.

- ◆ Avoid purchasing "vaporware" (untried software in development to be released in the future).

- ◆ Look to the financial health and stability of the selected vendor.

- ◆ Make sure the system includes productive tools, such as a good word-processing program.

- ◆ Give ample training to teachers who are to use the ILS (Trotter, 1990).

- ◆ Ensure that the ILS lab meets acceptable standards for comfort, safety, and utility.

- ◆ Determine if an ILS lab or distributed ILS network suits the building's needs.

TIPS-TRICKS-TRAPS

TIPS

| TIP #1 | A special edition of *Electronic Learning* (1992) listed several tips for the effective integration of an ILS. |

- ◆ Principals must be ILS leaders by modeling and creating excitement for the ILS with their teachers.

- Principals must help teachers overcome reluctance based on "technophobia."

- Principals must hold regular in-service workshops for teachers, to demonstrate the features of an ILS.

- Principals should hire competent ILS managers who have instructional backgrounds.

- Principals should ensure that the reports generated by an ILS are used to communicate with parents and modify educational programming.

- Principals should provide correlational charts for the ILS and the instructional curriculum.

TIP #2

Carefully investigate the financial background of the ILS corporation being considered. Principals do not want to make a major purchase of an ILS system with a firm that is about to go out of business.

TIP #3

Order more printers. They will be used.

TRICKS

TRICK #1

Principals can build enthusiasm and perhaps generate funds for an ILS by providing adult literacy programs with the system during nonschool hours.

TRICK #2

Several ILS and software developers are producing third-party programs that run with an ILS management system. This gives teachers and principals expanded options when choosing software packages.

TRAPS

TRAP #1

Management systems can be extremely difficult to use. Having little support from the vendor can bring a well-planned ILS to a halt. Principals should investigate and compare management systems thoroughly before recommending purchase.

TRAP #2

Annual licensing or update fees for ILS software can be expensive. Investigate and plan for these costs as an ongoing expense.

TRAP #3 An ILS purchased exclusively with Chapter 1 or disadvantaged moneys may have to be dedicated solely to serving a specific class of students.

EXAMPLES

WRITING TO READ

In a large-scale California demonstration project to evaluate the *Writing to Read* program (IBM Corporation), four networked computers were used in kindergarten and first-grade classrooms. Networking the computers freed students from having to work with disks and allowed them to log on independently throughout the school day. Teachers developed daily lesson units tailored to specific needs of students. Networked software was made available to support classroom goals. Several instruments for evaluation were used. These included classroom observations, pre- and post-test scores from reading aptitude surveys, yearlong portfolios, interviews, and questionnaires. The major conclusions of this study were that students had more positive attitudes toward reading and writing, and greater success than those in traditional classrooms (Anderson-Inman, 1994).

INTEGRATING AN ILS: TWO TEACHING MODELS THAT WORK

In one model for using an integrated learning system, the computers are centralized in one location. Students leave the regular classroom to work in the ILS lab. This school is committed to achieving an outcomes-based curriculum. The teachers first endorsed the curriculum and later bought into using an ILS as a means of providing this curriculum.

A second model for an ILS distributed the equipment throughout the classrooms. Teachers retain greater control over the ILS and the students' learning. During the early phases of this distribution teachers used the ILS as another classroom resource, not the central part of the curriculum. It was not until later that instructional delivery through the ILS became central to the classroom educational program (Mageau, 1992).

PROJECT CHILD

By combining altered instruction scheduling with an ILS, the Florida-based Project CHILD created a new program for integrating instructional technology with regular classroom teaching. Three classrooms formed a CHILD cluster. Each teacher became a content specialist in addition to working with one class. Each of the classrooms are organized with ILS learning stations appropriate for the teacher's content specialty. The software provided with the program encourages higher-order thinking and applied learning skills. An essential part of this program is daily use of the technology. Project CHILD has been validated by the Program Effectiveness Panel of the U.S. Department of Education's National Diffusion Network (Butzin, 1992).

ILS: ITS NEW ROLE IN SCHOOLS

A California school with nearly 70 percent of its students from a minority population and nearly 60 percent of the students living below the poverty line posted impressive academic achievements. The district administration attributes their high rate of success to a districtwide commitment to an integrated learning system. Installed in every K–1 classroom in this district is an IBM *Writing to Read* lab. Each 2–6 grade classroom has three IBM PS/2 Model 25 computers connected to a distributed network. The file servers carry Wasatch Educational System software for language arts, math, and science. Also included in the network software are learning tools for students, including a word processor, glossary, notebook calculator, graphing program, and electronic mail. This equipment and software were all purchased with state and local moneys and IBM grants; no Chapter 1 funds were used (Mageau,1990).

THE SATURN SCHOOL

The Saturn School was established to blend the best methods of existing schools with powerful emerging technologies. Access to technology plays a key role for teachers and students in establishing an individualized learning environment. Teachers focus on individual students by using integrated learning systems, as well as stand-alone software. Both Jostens and Computer Curriculum Corporation's ILSs are in place. The Jostens system presents information using color graphics and video. The Computer Curriculum Corporation system is more straightforward and responsive to the learner's performance (Hopkins,1991).

Recommended Readings for Chapter 6:
Integrated Learning Systems

Bailey, G. D. (ed.) (1992). *Computer-Based Integrated Learning Systems*. Englewood Cliffs, NJ: Educational Technology Publications.

Electronic Learning. (1991). Integrated Learning Systems: How to buy an ILS. *Electronic Learning*, Special supplement, Winter, 1991, 6–12.

Finkel, L. (1992). Are ILSes Worth the $$? *Electronic Learning, 12*(1), 18.

Sherry, M. (1990). Implementing an Integrated Instructional System. *Phi Delta Kappan, 72*(2), 118–120.

White, M. A. (1989). Educators Must Ask Themselves Some Important Questions. *Electronic Learning, 9*(1), 6–7.

———. (1992). Are ILSs Good Education? *Educational Technology, 32*(9), 49–50.

CHAPTER 7

Electronic Collaborative Learning

Electronic collaborative learning is a transformational methodology in which learners using networking strategies work together as teams on projects over time and distance.

> *The next breakthrough won't be in the individual interface but in the team interface.*
>
> JOHN SEELY BROWN

KEY QUESTION

How can technology help schools develop student learning teams?

OVERVIEW

CONCEPT

Using electronic network and display technologies, learners work together to create, access, discover, and share information in collaborative efforts.

CENTER OF LEARNING CONTROL

In electronic collaborative learning, the learning team is the center of learning control.

DISCUSSION

Student cooperation and collaboration are not particularly new developments in teaching methodologies. Johnson and Johnson (1991) and Slavin (1983) outlined the essential features of cooperative learning. Their work centered on the development of cooperative learning teams as a strategy for enhancing educational opportunities for children. Johnson and Johnson and Slavin developed and tested models for improving student performance in the classroom by developing learning teams.

Educational network collaboration is a recent continuation of Johnson and Johnson's and Slavin's work. Electronic networks have created conditions that allow cooperation and collaboration in school settings. The design of electronic collaborative learning is to make "the boundaries between classrooms and class periods more permeable" (Newman, 1992, p. 312). Electronic collaboration allows students to work together on learning projects in different schools and at different times.

In the reality of educational practice, boundaries have been established that are both physical (walls and distance) and timely (class periods and school days). These boundaries have limited opportunities for cooperative learning to single classrooms and class periods. Electronic collaborative learning allows students to overcome these boundaries and work as teams over time and distance. The teacher facilitates and collaborates in the learning process.

"Cooperative learning is a structured process built on the belief that we learn better when we learn together" (Bruder, 1992a, p. 18). The SCANS report identified the ability to cooperatively work togerther as one of the crucial skills for the world of work in the year 2000 (U.S. Department Labor, 1991). Clearly, cooperation and collaboration are significant learning methods. Both maintain a strong emphasis on shared talents and group efforts toward learning common outcomes. Electronic networks support and expand these learning opportunities. They add power to cooperative and collaborative learning, transforming them into new and unique learning methods. These electronic networks and the skills to work together have become critical features of schooling in the Information Age.

A significant benefit of networking strategies within cooperative or collaborative learning environments is the opportunity for students to interact over both time and distance. Students no longer have to be face-to-face to work collaboratively or cooperatively. They can be in different buildings, towns, or countries, and meet at different times.

PAYOFFS

Johnson and Johnson (1991) and Slavin (1983) noted positive outcomes for cooperative learning in both the cognitive and affective domains. These positive outcomes included significant cognitive achievement in problem solving and group production. In the affective domain, attitudes toward instructional activities, self-esteem, and intergroup relations improved. Electronic technologies add dimension to these cooperative benefits by allowing cooperative learning over time and space. Johnson and Johnson (1985) listed that, when working together on a computer, students could:

- Observe and imitate each other's use of the computer

- Observe, imitate, and build upon each other's strategies, thereby increasing mastery

- Experience the encouragement, support, warmth, and approval of classmates

- Have peers evaluate, diagnose, correct, and give feedback on understanding

- Have greater exposure to diverse ideas and procedures

- Develop more critical thinking and more creative responses

Adding to Johnson and Johnson's outcomes of cooperative learning, Schrage (1990) listed benefits of technology through enhanced media that integrates the intellectual virtues of print, the appeal of television, and the information-handling power of computers. To Schrage, the media may be the message, but collaboration redefined the meaning of both media and message.

STRATEGIES

There are several strategies for electronic collaborative and cooperative learning. The essential nonelectronic features of these have been outlined by Slavin (1983) and Johnson and Johnson (1991).

Recognizing Johnson and Johnson's efforts, how can technology enhance student cooperative learning? Four strategies seem most appropriate for maximizing the benefits of electronic cooperative or collaborative learning over time and space: same time–same place, same time–different place, different time–same place, and different time–different place (R. Johnson, 1991).

SAME TIME–SAME PLACE

Students in the same classroom work together with the equipment in discovering or creating course materials. Face-to-face electronic collaborative learning uses technology to develop solutions to group problems. Students can share display devices (monitors and LCD panels) or input devices (keyboards and electronic pointers).

SAME TIME–DIFFERENT PLACE

In this strategy, learners work at different places, connected by electronic networks. These learners may be across the nation, across town, or across the hall. They may be connected by a phone line, microwave tower, or satellite. All students meet at the same time but at different places to develop products or understandings. Wide area networks (WAN) may be employed to work with students across the nation. Local area networks (LAN) can be used by students to collaborate with students in the next classroom.

DIFFERENT TIME–SAME PLACE

In this strategy, learners work together on the same project, on the same workstations, but at different times to meet the needs of their individual lifestyles. Work-stations or terminals store team members' work for later reference by other members of the team. A LAN allows students to store electronic documents on a network server for other students to work on at a later time. Electronic mail (E-mail) is a common communication technology of this strategy.

DIFFERENT TIME-DIFFERENT PLACE

In this strategy, information is developed and forwarded for electronic collaborative learning to other locales to be worked on later. This strategy appears to be a useful technique when collaboratively learning over distance and through several time zones. Terminals are connected electronically and have the ability to store team members' progress.

STAFF

Staff electronic collaboration is an important element in electronic collaborative learning, beneficial for teachers as well as students. Teacher isolation has been identified as one factor retarding the development of common instructional goals (Goodlad, 1984). Teachers, as well as students, can use electronic mail and other similar technologies to overcome the "isolation factor" of educational programs. Teachers, electronically connected over networks, develop and share with colleagues across the hall or across town. These teachers find electronic networks to be invaluable resources for improving instructional programming. Teachers find they can professionally communicate with each other more effectively if they have networking capabilities in their classrooms (McREL, 1992). Administrative burdens—such as attendance, grade reporting and accounting—can be lightened through electronic building or district networks.

To employ electronic collaborative and cooperative learning strategies, teachers need a firm grasp of cooperative and collaborative learning without technology. They can weld electronic technology to these models to improve and expand opportunities for student collaboration.

Networking computers involves a complex series of technological skills that must be mastered for teachers to effectively communicate. These skills appear to be:

- ◆ Basic computer operation
- ◆ Shared computer operation over a LAN with a dedicated server
- ◆ Electronic mail
- ◆ Understanding of a modem or other computer communication device

Grunwald (1991) outlined an eight-step plan to provide for instructional networking in the classroom.

1. Provide telephone lines.

2. Provide hardware.

3. Provide software.

4. Consider standardizing software.

5. Select and budget for services.

6. Provide initial training.

7. Encourage use.

8. Provide ongoing training.

What should principals look for in teachers using electronic collaborative learning technology methods?

- ◆ Ability to manage cooperative learning activities.

- ◆ Collaboration of teachers over time and distance.

- ◆ Sharing of scarce data-management resources.

- ◆ Aid in creating a common school culture through staff communication.

- ◆ Encouraging students to develop collaborative and cooperative skills electronically.

- ◆ A movement away from whole-class instruction toward more collaborative work in small groups (Newman, 1992).

STUDENTS

Given sufficient training and equipment, electronic collaborative learning provides an effective learning method for a wide range of students. Special emphasis has been placed on these methods for children with exceptionalities. With growing diversity in the classroom, electronic network technologies hold extra promise for incorporating exceptional children into the mainstream classroom (Male, 1986). The very uniqueness of these students adds to the value of the electronic cooperative and collaborative projects. Linda Roberts, a senior associate of the U. S. Congress Office of

Technology and Assessment, expressed a firm conviction that telecommunications greatly expanded both the quality and quantity of information resources available in the classroom (Leslie, 1993).

Classroom network activities need to be well structured. Specific rules for collaboration and discussion must be clearly spelled out and enforced. Controls must be set to ensure that all students have opportunities to express themselves yet not dominate equipment or the communication lines. Group and individual assessment plans must also be clearly spelled out.

What should principals look for in students using electronic collaborative learning technology methods?

- ◆ Collaboration over time and distance.

- ◆ Increased ability to access and analyze data.

- ◆ Ability to use electronic technology to work together to achieve common goals.

- ◆ Increased acceptance of other students from different backgrounds and cultures.

FACILITIES

Facility planning for electronic collaborative or cooperative learning stations has several aspects, depending upon the strategy desired.

CLASSROOM COLLABORATIVE AND COOPERATIVE LEARNING STATIONS

When learning stations are set up in the classroom, students work in small groups. They often share developments on a common display screen. This pattern follows guidelines associated with the Johnson and Johnson model (1985, 1991). Students can electronically access other students, the instructor, and learning materials. In some manner all students see the same work, whether be through a large-screen monitor, projection device, or common screen shown on each student's monitor. The important feature of this classroom network is that students have connectivity and opportunities to enhance the developing product.[1]

---

[1] See Transparency ECL 1 for a diagram to help explain this facility modification to stakeholders.

COOPERATION AND COLLABORATION
OUTSIDE THE CLASSROOM

A crucial feature of this method is the connective wiring. Communicative devices must be connected through some sort of network, telecommunication, or modem devices that allow sharing of data. In planning for this type of distribution and cooperation, there is no substitute for speed of transmission. Speed of transmission becomes increasingly important as video and sound become shared resources for teachers and learners.

The volume of data that can be transmitted is often expressed as *bandwidth*. As networking strategies begin supporting increasingly complex multimedia applications, the bandwidth required for effective transmission increases geometrically. For example, ordinary telephone service requires a transmission speed of 2–10 kbps (kilobits per second). High-quality compressed video requires a transmission speed of 6–24 mbps (megabits per second) (Hargadon, 1992).[2] Transparency ECL 2 was developed to indicate to the novice the complexities of the almost geometric increases in speed and bandwidth required by new video technologies. As more and more data is transmitted, faster and wider transmission technologies are required.

TOPOLOGY

The layout, or *topology*, of electronic networks is a special consideration for school administrators. Building and campus structures often impact the network topology. Topology has important implications for the curriculum infrastructure of student networking capabilities.

- ◆ **STAR TOPOLOGY** network devices are connected by lines branching from a central node or server (Motorola Codex, 1992). These "stars" radiate outward from a central location and may subdivide into other stars or "bridge" to other networks. The central node constitutes a single point of failure or maintenance. Expansion of the network does not disrupt other working devices, but transmission from outlying devices can be slowed as the network becomes larger.[3]

- ◆ **BUS OR BACKBONE TOPOLOGY** network devices are connected along a high-speed, wide-bandwidth central cable. These devices must be addressable (know their own address). Expansion requires no rewiring, and no single node failure causes network failure (Motorola Codex, 1992).[4]

- ◆ **RING OR TOKEN-RING TOPOLOGY** devices are connected in a circle. Each device acts as a repeater along the network. Control

---

[2] See Transparency ECL 2 for a diagram of bandwidth requirements for communication.

[3] See Transparency ECL 3 for a diagram to help explain this topology to significant stakeholders.

[4] See Transparency ECL 4 for a diagram to help explain this topology to significant stakeholders.

of the network is distributed, but any failure along the ring causes the whole network to collapse. Expansion of the network requires interruption since the ring must be temporarily broken to accommodate the installation of new nodes (Motorola Codex, 1992).[5]

Few facility improvements are needed to connect to an off-site information service—only a computer, modem, phone line, and telecommunications software package. Dedicated phone lines are recommended (Eiser, 1990). Planning for future installations may indicate fiber-optic networks. Fiber-optic lines have the capability of transmitting at speeds and bandwidths that will allow for full-motion video.

BUDGET

The budget for electronic cooperative and collaborative learning can be as extensive or minimal as desired. For example, FrEd Mail, started in 1984 and now serving 10,000 classrooms and 500,000 students, is free (Leslie, 1993). Factors to be considered in adoption are:

- ◆ Communication terminals (computers)

- ◆ Required connective devices (modems, cards)

- ◆ Required wiring

- ◆ Display devices for sharing documents

- ◆ Specific instructor training

- ◆ Furniture to establish collaborative and cooperative classrooms

- ◆ Software for electronic mail or groupware

- ◆ Telephone-line charges

- ◆ Access charges to databases

- ◆ A dedicated server

---

[5] See Transparency ECL 5 for a diagram to help explain this topology to significant stakeholders.

TIPS-TRICKS-TRAPS

TIPS

TIP #1
One of the most effective ways of encouraging faculty use of technology and improving school communications is through electronic mail. Electronic mail not only helps the technophobic teacher get accustomed to computers, but it also enhances school communication.

TIP #2
Installing a mini-network of computers in adjacent rooms allows students to practice cooperative and collaborative skills without meeting face-to-face. This strategy parallels some of the same ways business teams work on projects.

TRICKS

TRICK #1
Corresponding with electronic pen pals is a good way for students to experience foreign cultures and practice language skills in foreign-language classes.

TRICK #2
Networking with community resources (e.g., libraries and government agencies) provides valuable access for the school to these resources, and the public can increase the use of taxpayer-supported school resources.

TRAPS

TRAP #1
Schools wishing to use videotape technology with foreign students find the formats of American video (NTSC) and European video (PAL) incompatible.

TRAP #2
Schools often purchase cheaper, slower modems. The purchase of faster, higher-priced modems is quickly recovered by lower telephone charges.

TRAP #3
Data-transmission wiring is a technical and complex subject. Schools often purchase wiring with insufficient bandwidth to effectively transmit the data they wish to send. Principals planning for both present and anticipated networking needs may wish to contract qualified system engineers to design their school network system.

TRAP #4 Both security and the lack of security on a network can be the source of grief for school principals. A balance between ease of use and privacy must be planned and implemented as the network is being installed. Network security planning must involve at least three issues:

1. Protection from viruses.

2. Unauthorized access to confidential files.

3. Unlawful duplication of software.

EXAMPLES

A BIOSPHERE RESEARCH EXPEDITION

Three New York junior high schools, scientific experts, and student cooperative teams are linked together by electronic mail. This collaborative group created a research project to design a life-sustaining biosphere. Students use scanners and computers to develop plans for the biosphere. They then exchange the biosphere examples they have developed with colleagues using an electronic network. Likewise, they critique colleagues' designs for scientific accuracy using the same network. The instructor feels the program promotes greater student research, student independent learning, and student networking (Reissman,1992).

LIGHTS, CAMERAS...STUDENTS

At a Florida school, teams of students are known as the "knowledge producers." These student teams get together each morning to create their own news program, which is broadcast over the school's video system. These students don't just watch TV; they make it. As a result of this collaboration, these students have become more aware of themselves and others within the school. In addition to using their TV network for school news, the students present dramas, interview guests, and give tips on a variety of topics (Hutchins, 1993).

WHAT GOT ME HOOKED

National Geographic Kids Network, an on-line network of specific lessons, brings history and geography into elementary classrooms. Students from around the world come together electronically to conduct research on timely topics, including acid rain, solar energy, and water pollution. Students collect data locally and exchange it internationally to make global connections (Novelli, 1993).

BETTER TOOLS FOR BETTER TEAMWORK

A variety of technology tools are used in a classroom of mixed-ability students to help the teacher meet the needs and celebrate the strengths of all students. Learning centers were developed to foster cooperation among the students. These centers contain computers, video cameras, and mini-keyboards. Students use this equipment to collaboratively author a new type of student project or product (Novelli, 1993).

PEOPLE-TO-PEOPLE

"Keypals" is a common use of wide-area networking for student-to-student or group-to-group exchange. One example is a well-structured class from a suburban school in Pennsylvania. In a call for participation, a sixth-grade class asked to exchange cultural information with educators and their students in foreign countries. Using FrEd Mail, these sixth graders exchanged biographical, geographical, historical, political, social, religious, and environmental information with foreign counterparts (Harris, 1994).

THE EARTH DAY TREASURE HUNT

Upper elementary and middle school students from around the country participate in a treasure hunt using telecommunications. Participating classrooms submit, by electronic mail, clues describing a geographical place. On Earth Day the clues are downloaded and students investigate a wide variety of places throughout the world. As it is an Earth Day activity, environmental clues are especially encouraged. Students get excited about developing clues for their locale and attempt to respond to the search clues provided by other students (Burry, 1993).

GALAXY CLASSROOM

The schools participating in the Galaxy program set up a satellite dish, television, and fax machine to allow students to collaborate with fellow second graders across the nation. Central to the curriculum of the Galaxy activity is a series of television dramas dealing with a variety of issues that students respond to using a telephone line and fax machine. Students often see their work appear on subsequent episodes of the television program. Evaluation of the program has found that Galaxy students' reading scores are nearly double those of nonparticipating control groups (Graumann, 1994).

LEARNING WITH COMPUTERS

More than 40 schools in several different countries participated in an international newspaper day. News articles were exchanged via electronic mail and edited into school newspapers around the world. Students spent weeks preparing the manuscripts and learning the techniques necessary to submit articles via a modem to an international network. Student excitement for the project grew as they observed their own work appearing on the international bulletin board. In one city, 20,000 copies of an eight-page tabloid were printed and distributed (Ryba and Anderson, 1993).

Recommended Readings for Chapter 7: Electronic Collaboration Learning

Johnson, D. W., and R. T. Johnson (1985). Cooperative Learning: One key to computer-assisted learning. *The Computing Teacher, 13*(1), 11–13.

Johnson, R. (1991). *Leading Business Teams: How teams can use technology and groups process tools to enhance performance.* Reading, MA: Addison-Wesley.

Motorola Codex (1992). *The Basics Book of Information Networking.* Reading, MA: Addison-Wesley.

Schrage, M. (1990). *Shared Minds: The new technologies of collaboration.* New York: Random House.

Slavin, R. E. (1983). *Cooperative Learning.* New York: Longman.

CHAPTER 8

Hyperlearning

*Hyperlearning is a
transformational methodology in
which students are in charge
of their own learning and teachers
serve as guides and coaches.*

KEY QUESTION

**How can schools help students become self-directed
learners who are capable of evaluating, organizing,
maintaining, interpreting, communicating,
and processing information electronically?**

OVERVIEW

CONCEPT

Hyperlearning allows learners using electronic technologies to learn, explore, and
author in nonlinear ways.

CENTER OF LEARNING CONTROL

In hyperlearning, the individual student is the center of learning control.

DISCUSSION

Hyperlearning was used by Perelman (1992) to express a view calling for the end
of formal schooling. The concept of hyperlearning contains a philosophy that control
of the learning process passes from the teacher to the student. This handbook recognizes schools as educational institutions, but hyperlearning environments radically
alter the role of students and teachers.

Because of the difficulties in grasping hyperlearning concepts and confusion about
terminology, some operational definitions have been inserted to help the reader.

Hypertext (and in a broader sense, *hypermedia*) is a knowledge-representation system composed of nodes of information on a nonlinear framework (Dede, 1988).

Data is input gathered by the senses (Dede, 1988).

Information is integrated data that denotes a significant change in the environment (Dede, 1988).

Knowledge is information converted through interconnection to known concepts and skills.

Wisdom is knowledge about knowledge (Dede, 1988).

Vanaver Bush (1945) and Ted Nelson (1987) envisioned a technology process where learners explore vast fields of information. In the Bush and Nelson example, each learner controls the learning process. Recently, Thomas Armstrong (1993) related this nonlinear learning model with electronic technologies to match students' cognitive strengths. In an appendix, Armstrong listed specific types of software to match individual intelligences.

Hyperlearning presumes knowledge is cross-connected in a wide array of manners (Nelson, 1987). Hyperlearning is based on a philosophy of easy access to large bodies of information (Rezabek, 1989). In hyperlearning, learners are responsible for directing their own learning (Jonassen, 1989). This self-directed learning imposes new responsibilities on both teachers and students. Hyperlearning has a strong background in the constructivist learning theories of Piaget and Papert (1980, 1991).

Principals should realize that hyperlearning can also take place using a print medium, such as a thesaurus, as a paper version of hypertext. However, electronic technologies allow explorers of any subject matter to quickly leap from topic to topic within electronic documents or information sources. Traditional methods of arranging material from beginning to end may no longer be necessary, or the best way of teaching.

Because learning is centered on the learners' interests, the role of the teacher in hyperlearning is one of guiding students. Teachers are no longer the sole providers of material and direction for learning. The teacher's role becomes one of suggester, prompter, and partner. This new role for teachers is different from the traditional method of dispensing predigested knowledge in a sequential, measured fashion to passive students.

PAYOFFS

Specific outcomes are difficult to measure in hyperlearning. Assessment strategies in hyperlearning are still subject for original research and debate. However, some characteristics and fields of research are encouraging.

- ◆ Hyperlearning provides easy access to huge collections of information in a variety of media.

- ◆ Hyperlearning provides students with an enabling environment rather than a directive one.

- Hyperlearning provides altered roles for teachers and students.

- Hyperlearning provides increased learner abilities in higher-order thinking skills (Marchionini, 1988).

STRATEGIES

In hyperlearning there are two strands: exploring and authoring. Together they form a core for understanding hyperlearning educational strategies.

Hyperlearning exploring occurs when learners browse and roam through information sources seeking material interesting to them. Learners search rich data sources for chunks of information having meaning, connection, and interest. In exploring through hyperlearning environments, students construct unique meanings. In hyperlearning, a student's understanding has value because the material is connected to already acquired knowledge or experience. Students learn because the learning has meaning for them, not because a teacher tells them "it will be good for you." Learners build connections to material that interests them. They construct scaffolds or webs to build upon and connect to previously held knowledge.

Authoring and exploring are closely connected in hyperlearning. Because students explore in ways interesting to them, they are simultaneously authoring and exploring. In choosing pieces of data to include in their collection of information, students author for themselves. Authoring in hyperlearning is exploring, and exploring in hyperlearning is authoring.

MULTIMEDIA EXPLORING

Multimedia is a strategy often associated with hyperlearning. The term *hypermedia* is a combination of *hyper*text and multi*media*. *Hyper* implies nonlinear. *Multimedia* denotes the use of many media forms of communication: sound, animation, video, graphics, and still images. As a strategy, learners create or interact with nonlinear projects and demonstrate their understanding through the use of multimedia. *Odysseys* © (IBM) is an example of hypermedia. In this project, learners explore Homer's epic poem in a nonlinear fashion, using text, sound, graphics, and video.

HYPERTEXT EXPLORING

Hypertext is usually, but not always, an electronic document for individual learner exploration. These documents contain a variety of media: text, graphics, sound, etc. Learners leap from one section to another depending on their particular interests, just as, traditionally, a student browses through an encyclopedia following his or her own interests. Electronic hypertext exploring is shown by *Culture*© (Cultural Resources) and *Timeline©* (MECC). In these packages, students explore electronic text documents linking art, music, and history.

HYPERLEARNING EXPLORING VIA NETWORK

If connected by a modem and a phone line, learners interested in their own discovery can access immense sources of information. From these resources, they gather data suitable for their own learning. They have the power to use these sources of information to create an understanding for themselves and knowledge for others. This strategy was envisioned by Ted Nelson (1987) in *Xanadu* and is practiced by learners searching both publicly owned networks (e.g., *Internet*) and commercial networks (e.g., *Prodigy®*).

HYPERLEARNING AUTHORING

Learners author nonlinear documents, using either text or media. These documents express their understanding but allow for a variety of interests. Authoring tools for this process are *HyperCard©* (Claris), *Linkway Live©* (IBM), and *Guide©* (Owl). These authoring tools are more than word processors. They connect nodes of information by associative links. Moreover, these programs use other electronic documents, such as laserdisks, to present data and information in an interactive way. If electronically connected to other hyperlearners, authors can collaboratively develop hyperlearning documents.

STAFF

The teacher's role in a hypertextual learning environment changes as radically as the students' role. Rather than addressing students from a position as sage-on-the-stage, the teacher becomes a guide-on-the-side. Rather than being the source of all learning, teachers become counselors in student exploration of the vast field of knowledge. The teacher's role is to aid students in reflection about their own learning. Teachers engaging in hyperlearning methods must develop a new set of highly sophisticated skills. These skills include: a broader and deeper understanding of subject domains, new methods of questioning, suggesting paths for exploration, and helping students construct their own understanding.

Jonassen (1986) noted learner control is based on two assumptions: 1) learners know what is best for them at any given time, and 2) learners are capable of acting appropriately on this knowledge. The teacher's role becomes one of enabling learners to fulfill these two assumptions.

What should principals look for when observing teachers using hyperlearning methods?

- ◆ Nontraditional methods of evaluation, which include electronic portfolios, standards negotiated between teacher and student, evaluation based on learner reflection.

- ◆ Learners developing their own goals for learning.

- ◆ Teachers as guides on the side.

STUDENTS

The student role in a hyperlearning methodology is significantly different from that in past educational methods. Rather than acting as passive recipients of information flowing from teacher to student, students become active participants in creating their own learning. In advanced hyperlearning methods, individual students determine what to explore, what knowledge interests them, what medium of expression suits their intelligence, and in what time frame they want it presented. Empowerment for students becomes a real possibility for student-directed learning.

Empowerment of students in hyperlearning methods challenges many fundamental assumptions of reforms calling for greater uniformity and standards of educational accomplishment. The material to be examined is determined by the student. The standards for success are accomplished not in relationship to national norms, but in relationship to the needs of the student and future employers. This newfound freedom of students to explore and develop their own learning comes with a heavy responsibility. Student-directed learning provokes new standards for evaluation, which include student self-assessment, electronic portfolios, and demonstration projects.

What should principals look for when observing students using hyperlearning technology methods?

- ◆ A new, nonlinear method of authoring.

- ◆ Technical skills involving multimedia.

- ◆ Increased enthusiasm for student-directed learning.

- ◆ Learning attached to each student's previously known material.

- ◆ Inquisitive exploration of topics by students.

- ◆ Students' examination of their own learning process.

FACILITIES

Principals seeking to institute hyperlearning models in their buildings usually find specific facility requirements to be less of a problem than with other technology-based learning methods. Hypertext and hypermedia are more a state of mind than a concrete structural development. Hyperlearning relies more on attitudes about student-centered learning than on a large investment in equipment or facilities.

Hyperlearning can make advantageous use of other technological developments that would require extensive facilities modification. However, extensive facility modification is not required. One stand-alone computer with a minimum of software and an enthusiastic teacher and students is the start of hyperlearning. Specialized equipment for this type of instruction includes:

HYPERTEXT:

- ◆ Computer
- ◆ Specialized software

HYPERMEDIA:

- ◆ Computer
- ◆ Equipment for multimedia (e.g., video, laser disc audio, graphic, CD-ROM, etc.)

BUDGET

The budget for hyperlearning is small compared with other technology applications because equipment required and facilities modification are minimal. Depending upon the computer platform selected by the school district, one or two software packages can start a hyperlearning program.

TIPS-TRICKS-TRAPS

TIPS

TIP #1

Principals and teachers should establish clearly negotiated goals for student projects at the start of the project development. This avoids confusion and acrimony at the end of the project.

TIP #2

Principals and teachers should involve parents at the outset of a hyperlearning project to enlist their support and ensure they clearly understand the goals and purposes of the project.

TIP #3

Principals and teachers should initiate a public-relations effort with the media about new learning strategies involving hyperlearning. If the community and significant stakeholders are unclear about the goals and techniques of hyperlearning at the start of such a project, a misconception can develop that students are just doing their own thing while the teachers no longer teach.

TRICKS

TRICK #1

Students practice writing hyperlearning with flowcharts, storyboards, and different endings to fairy tales. At a young age, students can start to explore authoring in a nonlinear fashion.

TRICK #2

Instructors are thoroughly trained in both the electronic skills and their new roles as guides on the side. The key to this trick is training teachers to use new methods of instruction and to perceive new roles for themselves in the teaching and learning process. More than just a basic technical skill in new equipment is necessary for the change in attitude and practice that must accompany this equipment for effective hyperlearning to take place.

TRICK #3

Workshops and activities for the faculty on constructivist philosophies and learning techniques are scheduled. Faculty must be made aware of recent advances in constructivist learning and cognitive psychology.

TRICK #4

Faculty and students can investigate assessment of hyperlearning products in ways similar to how traditional essays are assessed for grammar, content, style, and logical development. At the same time, new assessment strategies for hyperlearning products must be explored by teachers and students.

TRAPS

TRAP #1 Without strong guidance, hyperlearning projects lack meaningful substance. Because traditional methods of assessment are meaningless in hyperlearning, new forms of assessment must be carefully crafted at the outset.

TRAP #2 Measuring student achievement from hyperlearning projects with traditional standardized testing is destined for failure.

EXAMPLES

LEARNING BEYOND THE CLASSROOM

Westfield, Indiana, students, teachers, and parents established a high-tech network of computers, multimedia imaging equipment, and satellite technology to link the school with many information resources. They studied science, world history, politics, and current events by investigating resources linked to this network. Students were able to access and retrieve video programs and filmstrips through a school-based technology resource center. Teachers were able to create their own CD-Interactive discs for classroom instruction (*Electronic Learning, 12*(7), 1993).

MATHEMATICAL EXPLORATION IN LOGO

A pilot study of sixth-grade students engaged in mathematical explorations was carried out in the context of a national LOGO project in Costa Rica. Thirty-four students, approximately 12 years old, worked in pairs investigating a mathematical microworld written in LOGO. The investigation had three phases: 1) open exploration of the microworld, during which the students recorded their observations and formulated hypotheses about how the program worked; 2) group discussion and sharing of hypotheses; and 3) additional guided discovery and problem solving. The students were successful in discovering certain functions of their microworld during the first phase, but their hypotheses were improved after discussion with the instructor. The students were successful in applying their knowledge of the computer microworld in problem-solving tasks during the third phase (Edwards,1994).

HISTORY COMES ALIVE

Using *HyperCard*, a school district began to store information about the culture, language, and history of a local Native American tribe. Before the project was completed, the school was selling CD-ROM copies of the "Culture and History of the White Earth Ojibwe" for $20. The menu for exploration of this CD-ROM project included options for K–6 social studies, 7–9 social studies, natural resources, Native American poetry, language arts, Ojibwe leaders, Native American foods, civics, and classroom champions (Sterns, 1993).

LINKWAY FEATURES AND DESIGN

In an effort to help students clarify and define problems, students from San Francisco worked on the following problem:

> *Transportation is a matter of concern, especially in urban areas where growth is taking place. As a result of the 1989 Loma Prieta earthquake, a major artery through San Francisco, the Embarcadero Freeway, was closed, causing traffic congestion, as well as making Chinatown less accessible to tourists. Should the freeway be rebuilt?*

Students searched files of the *San Francisco Chronicle* and *San Jose Mercury*. These databases were found on Dialog's Classmate service. From their first set of articles, students formulated specific search questions involving the reconstruction of the freeway. In this on-line search activity, students focused on finding answers to real-life problems (Abramson, 1993).

Recommended Readings for Chapter 8: Hyperlearning

Bevilacqua, A. F. (1989). *Hypertext: Behind the hype.* (ERIC Document Reproduction Service No. ED 308 882).

Bush, V. (1945). The Way We May Think. *The Atlantic, 176*(1), 101–108.

Dede, C. (1987). Empowering Environments, Hypermedia and Microworlds. *The Computing Teacher, 15*(3) 20–24.

————. (1988). *The Role of Hypertext in Transforming Information into Knowledge.* NECC Conference, Dallas, TX 1988.

Jonassen, D. H. (1989). *Hypertext/Hypermedia.* Englewood Cliffs, NJ: Educational Technology Publications.

Nelson, T. (1987). *Computer Lib/Dream Machines.* Redmond, WA: Microsoft Press.

Papert, S. (1980). *Mindstorms: Children, computers, and powerful ideas.* New York: Basic Books, Inc.

Papert, S., and I. Harel (eds.) (1991). *Constructionism.* Norwood, NJ: Ablex.

Perelman, L. J. (1992). *School's Out: Hyperlearning, the new technology, and the end of education.* New York: William Morrow.

CHAPTER 9

Electronic Learning Simulations

Electronic learning simulation is a
restructuring methodology
in which technology is used to create
electronic learning scenarios.

KEY QUESTION

How can schools, using technology, help students understand systems for improving and correcting performance?

OVERVIEW

CONCEPT

In electronic learning simulations, students acquire concepts and understandings by interacting with scenarios produced by emerging electronic devices.

CENTER OF LEARNING CONTROL

The center of learning control is jointly held by the learner(s) and the computer.

DISCUSSION

Electronic simulation is an educational process in which students react to situations presented by software programming. These situations are designed to mirror real-life scenarios. Well-executed simulations provide a sense of life experience, and learning occurs through fundamental change in attitude and behavior (Henderson, 1991). Electronic simulation involves computing in a choice-laden environment. Electronic simulation often includes multimedia.

How does electronic simulation differ from other types of computer-assisted instruction (CAI)? CAI instruction involves students in learning detailed, decontextualized segments of information (e.g., math facts, states and state capitals, and the periodic table).

In electronic simulations, the learner makes decisions that affect the outcome of the simulation. Success or failure within the simulation is dependent not upon a student's learning a series of specific facts, but upon the student's ability to react and make choices from the responses relayed by the equipment.

Computer simulations for education imitate complex real-world situations. A common use in educational environments is for social studies and physical sciences. In social studies, students often role-play historical situations. In science they explore complex behavior of objects in Newtonian environments. These representations have been difficult to grasp by traditional means (U.S. Congress, Office of Technology Assessment, 1988).

Visionary principals see electronic simulations expanding into a new convergence of technologies (McLellan, 1991; Traub, 1991) called *virtual reality*. Virtual reality, a future extension of electronic simulation, is not yet practical or cost-effective for schools. Business, entertainment, and the military make great use of virtual reality and it will soon become available to schools (Reveaux, 1992). Principals may wish to keep up-to-date on virtual reality as it allows learners to enter computer-simulated, three-dimensional environments (Helsel, 1992; Hill, 1992; McClellan, 1991; Perelman, 1992).

PAYOFFS

Principals and teachers have difficulty documenting specific learning growth from electronic learning simulations with traditional methods of assessment. An electronic simulation may have a definite lesson to be learned (e.g., the pioneers' difficulties, the effects of cutting down the rain forest, or the results of economic policy designs). The objectives may be cognitive or they may be affective. The growth of each learner working with the simulation is difficult to document. Not all learners come away from the simulation with the same experience. If the simulation allows multiple paths and solutions, different learners will solve the problem in different ways. Most current test instruments are not designed to measure many different understandings.

Some payoffs may not be measurable by standardized tests. Among these are:

- ◆ Enthusiasm for learning by "playing a game"

- ◆ A greater depth of understanding by accessing several senses

- ◆ An affective understanding of complex topics studied by simulation

- ◆ A systems perspective through role-playing in simulations

STRATEGIES

SINGLE-LEARNER SIMULATION

Social studies class members take turns at the computer exploring, learning, and investigating with a simulation that matches the curriculum. Some popular programs for this strategy are *Oregon Trail©* (MECC), which investigates the difficulties of pioneers, and *Where in the World Is Carmen Sandiego©* (Broderbund), which takes students on a hunt for an arch-villain with clues from world geography.

In science, *Interactive Physics II©* (Knowledge Revolution) provides students with computer environments to simulate realistic motion. Using this program, students investigate planetary motion that may take years to occur. *Interactive Physics II* allows students to perform experiments in zero-gravity situations.

LEARNING-TEAM SIMULATION

Learners work in teams to solve problems generated by computer simulations. These simulations are often current social or environmental problems that present learners with the difficulties faced by real-world decision makers. Some examples are *SimCity©* and *SimEarth©* (Broderbund).

STAFF

Faculty understanding of electronic simulation is just now becoming a priority in education. Role-playing activities have been a technique in education for some time. However, the power to present a wide variety of branches in any solution, or to develop new options, which this new technology offers, encourages faculty members to develop more and more educational applications. In addition, assessment of educational accomplishment may be different for students who have availed themselves of different paths in the simulation.

What should principals look for in staff members using electronic learning simulations?

- ◆ Incorporation of electronic simulation into the curriculum.
- ◆ Authentic learning experiences developed for students using electronic simulations.

- Helping students, through electronic simulation, learn complex psychomotor skills that are dangerous or difficult to re-create in the real world.

- Electronic simulations reinforce and create new understandings of curriculum objectives.

STUDENTS

Learners in simulation activities understand a wide range of events. The learners develop a greater understanding of the complex interrelationships involved with science and social studies.

What should principals look for in students using electronic learning simulations?

- Deeper, empathetic understanding of course material.

- Improved decision-making skills.

- Improved collaborative skills.

- Improved psychomotor skills.

- Cooperative efforts to solve complex, real-life simulations.

FACILITIES

Principals planning facilities for electronic simulations need only provide a computer, a display screen, and a cart to carry this equipment.
Specialized equipment for simulation includes:

- Computer

- Specialized software

BUDGET

Principals whose schools possess relatively modern computer equipment find the cost of simulation software packages moderate. Many of these packages need little additional investment in hardware or staff training.

TIPS-TRICKS-TRAPS

TIPS

TIP #1
Students enjoy playing games. Electronic simulations often appear to be games in the eyes of students. Electronic simulations can be an exciting way to accomplish learning objectives.

TIP #2
Effective educators harness the competitiveness of students using electronic simulations. Teaming is an effective tactic. Teachers should ensure that all students have equal opportunity for success either individually or as part of a team.

TIP #3
Adventure games provide excellent opportunities for simulation to develop thinking skills. Students using adventure games can work in fantasy worlds or computer simulations of real worlds that offer them opportunities to explore and test a variety of problem-solving strategies (Ryba and Anderson, 1993).

TRICKS

TRICK #1
Many simulations work well on equipment that is becoming out-of-date. Use electronic simulations on this older equipment to reinforce and enhance the curriculum.

TRICK #2
Electronic simulations often imitate arcade-style games with sound, animation, and regular reinforcement.

TRAPS

Often simulations are used for reward and are unrelated to the curriculum. This is easy to spot. Students may use an electronic simulation for topics not being covered in the regular program of study. This leads to parental concerns about the kids just playing games at school rather than learning.

Given traditional time constraints in class, beware of electronic simulations that take hours to evolve. Also, because of their duration, these programs may not be able to sustain student interest.

Choosing an electronic simulation with motivational sound and graphics unsuitable to the age level of students can have a detrimental effect on student interest.

EXAMPLES

SCORE

Penn State University, with funding from AT&T, designed courseware for developing industry-specific skills for adults. The emphasis was on mid-literate adults who needed additional training in basic skills. The courseware (SCORE) uses simulations in a functional context to teach basic skills. Each simulation is in a highly visual scenario. Workers arrive at their simulated workspace, do the job, and are evaluated on their performance by a simulated supervisor. SCORE teaches basic workplace skills in math, reading, writing, problem solving, and critical thinking. Learners in this simulation sometimes work together in small groups to enhance teamwork and communication skills. At other times they work individually (Bixler and Spotts, 1994).

SAVE THE CITIES!

Using the game *SimCity*, 24 gifted students in a pull-out instructional program are introduced to an aspect of life they could not experience in their small town on a remote island in Alaska. They are introduced to the effects of decisions made by major metropolitan politicians. After their teacher takes them on a general walk-through of the program, the students are turned loose to run their simulated cities. Elementary school students are presented with the need to make critical, controversial decisions concerning taxes and city services (Jacobson, 1992).

PUTTING LIFE INTO COMPUTER-BASED TRAINING

Outbreak: Pharyngitis in Louisiana provides a realistic computer-based case study to simulate a disease outbreak in which students play the roles of lead investigator. This simulation, developed by the Center for Disease Control and Prevention, allows investigators to perform a variety of tasks related to the outbreak of a major disease threat. The major thrust of this simulation is to teach students how to conduct disease outbreak investigations. In the development of this simulation, three techniques are used to ensure that the simulations reflect real life as much as possible: realistic content portrayals, engaging graphics, and interactive teaching methods. Multiple outcomes are possible, depending upon the choices made during the course of the simulation (Gathany, and Stehr-Green, 1994).

OUTSIDE, A WORLD GOES BY

Using *Microsoft Flight Simulator*, 12- to 16-year-old students simulate real-world navigation problems using math skills they learn during regular instruction. This classroom simulation solidifies what they already know and teaches them to recognize the importance of the information and skills acquired during math. Students are encouraged to work as teams or whole classes on the simulated flights. A few advanced students are allowed to increase their skills and abilities in a simulation of their own. Ordinarily, students are asked to determine speed, time, distance, direction, and altitude in a group effort (van den Brink, 1994).

VIRTUAL BACK HOE

Beckman Institute for Advanced Science at the University of Illinois developed one of the first projects in virtual reality in a lab to develop skills in the operation of a backhoe. Trainees in backhoe operation have a virtual world displayed for them. This simulated world is analogous to the actual operation of a backhoe. The technological equipment involved in the virtual-reality simulation allows for portrayal of actual sight and sounds of backhoe operation. The sights are provided through the use of multiple cameras. The sound is conveyed through stereo headphones (NCSA Applications, 1994).

VIRTUAL REALITY LANDS THE JOB

When the Hubble Telescope failed to live up to its planned performance, the National Aeronautics and Space Administration set out on an ambitious plan to repair the telescope in space. In order to simulate the difficulties anticipated in such a complex operation, the repairs were practiced in a virtual-reality simulation at the Johnson Space Center. Each trainee wore a head-mounted display and an input glove. The simulator allowed movement around a simulated space shuttle payload bay, as though the trainee was in space. The director of the project said the virtual-reality simulation helped the men who repaired the shuttle understand procedures and equipment much better than they would have by studying traditional books, models, and diagrams (Delaney, 1994).

WHERE IN THE WORLD

Sixth-grade students use *Where in the World Is Carmen Sandiego?* as a simulation to help develop thinking skills. The students are grouped and given several sessions to play the adventure game. They record on a word processor all the clues they encounter. More than a thousand clues are collected and sorted into categories for printing. This database is also made available on a disk, and students are taught basic commands and how to retrieve information from a database. The students learn research skills in addition to learning how to use a word processor and a database. Their efforts are then shared with the entire school (Ryba and Anderson, 1993).

Recommended Readings for Chapter 9:
Electronic Learning Simulations

Helsel, S. K. (1990). *Interactive Optical Technologies in Education and Training.* Westport, CT: Meckler.

———. (1992). Virtual Reality as a Learning Medium. *Instructional Delivery Systems,* 6(4), 4–5.

Henderson, J. (1991). Designing Realities: Interactive media, virtual realities and cyberspace, in S. K. Helsel and J. P. Roth (eds.), *Virtual Reality: Theory, Practice and Promise 65–73.* Westport, CT: Meckler.

Lantz, E. (1992). Virtual Reality in Science Museums. *Instructional Delivery Systems,* 6(4), 10–12.

Perelman, L. J. (1992). *School's Out: Hyperlearning, the new technology, and the end of education.* New York: William Morrow.

PART III

Implementing Technology-Based Learning

CHAPTER 10

Technology Adoption Model

The technology adoption model provides a step-by-step process for implementing selected technology-based learning methods.

KEY QUESTIONS

Is there a model or pattern to aid in the implementation process of technology-based learning methods?

How, in a step-by-step process, do principals go about installing chosen technology-based learning methods?

This section is devoted to providing principals with a model for installing a selected technology-based learning method (TLM). Principals, in cooperation with significant stakeholders, may select one or more technology-based learning methods for their school. In pursuit of their educational goals, principals and significant stakeholders choose learning methods and appropriate strategies for teachers and students. The essential question is: How, in a step-by-step process, do principals go about installing a chosen TLM in their building? This section provides a model to answer that question.

A DECISION-MAKING FLOWCHART: TECHNOLOGY ADOPTION MODEL (TAM)

KEY QUESTION

How do principals go about installing a selected TLM in their building?

The technology adoption model (TAM) (see Figure 4) helps principals see the process for installing a new technology-based learning method. The process outlined by the TAM begins with investigation of a technology-based learning method (TLM) and ends at the beginning with investigation of another TLM for adoption. The TAM diagrams these decisions, along with several stop points, throughout the implementation process.

These stop points halt the progress toward district implementation at that level. Decisions involving stop do not necessarily indicate abandonment of the TLM. A stop point may be for modification of that method at that level. At a stop point principals and their planning teams may decide to implement the TLM at only their level, while other principals and their planning teams may choose different TLMs.

Figure 4

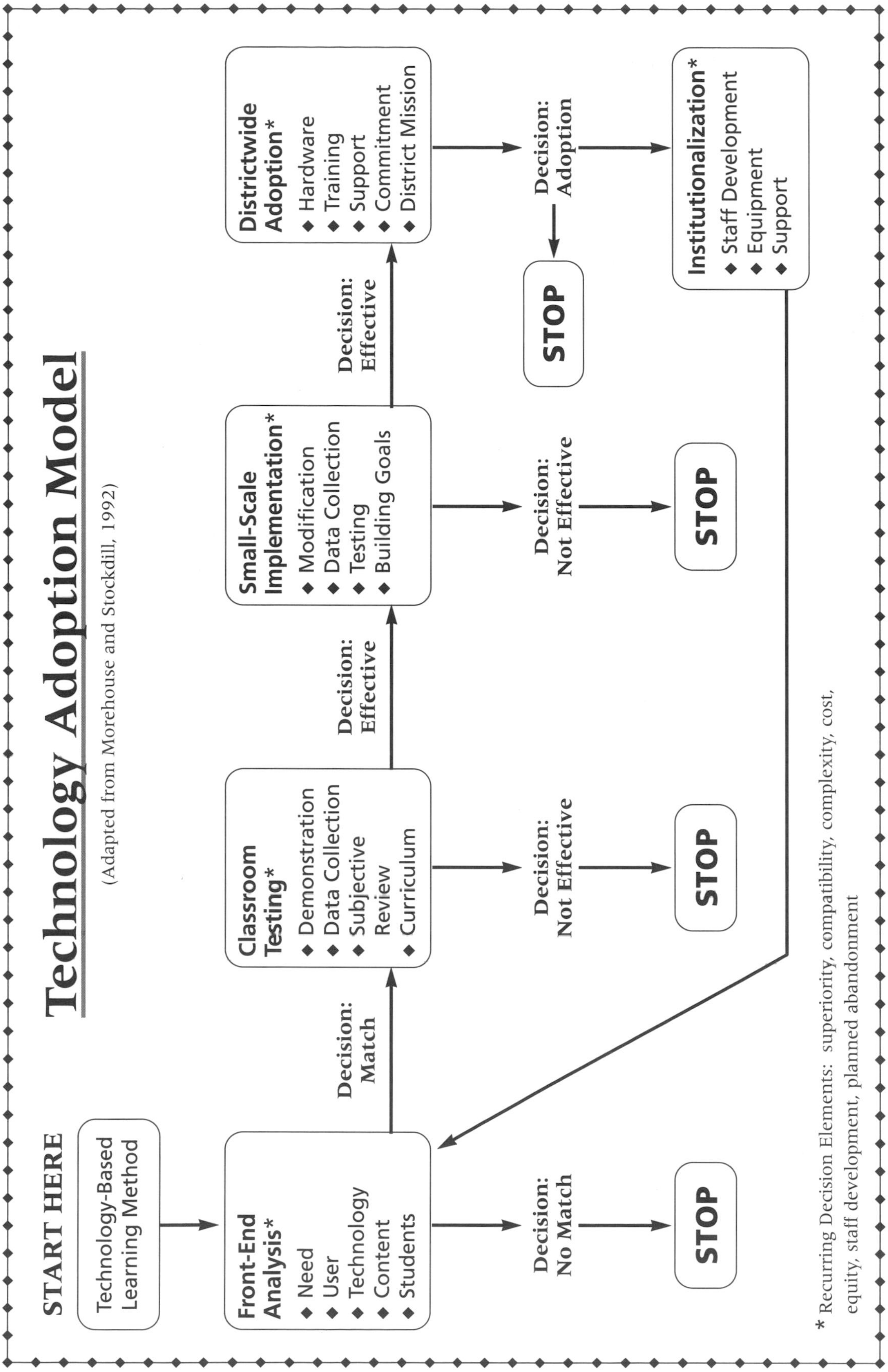

Technology Adoption Model

(Adapted from Morehouse and Stockdill, 1992)

START HERE

Technology-Based Learning Method

Front-End Analysis*
- Need
- User
- Technology
- Content
- Students

Decision: No Match → **STOP**

Decision: Match

Classroom Testing*
- Demonstration
- Data Collection
- Subjective Review
- Curriculum

Decision: Not Effective → **STOP**

Decision: Effective

Small-Scale Implementation*
- Modification
- Data Collection
- Testing
- Building Goals

Decision: Not Effective → **STOP**

Decision: Effective

Districtwide Adoption*
- Hardware
- Training
- Support
- Commitment
- District Mission

Decision: Adoption → **STOP**

Institutionalization*
- Staff Development
- Equipment
- Support

* Recurring Decision Elements: superiority, compatibility, complexity, cost, equity, staff development, planned abandonment

FIGURE 4: *Technology Adoption Model*

KEY QUESTION

What decisions must be made for any technology-based learning method?

There are seven recurring decision elements in each stage of the TAM. They are 1) superiority, 2) compatibility, 3) complexity, 4) cost, 5) equity, 6) staff development, and 7) planned abandonment. Each of these recurring decision elements of the TAM poses specific questions to be addressed by principals interested in technological implementation. Principals seeking to effectively install TLMs in their educational setting must respond positively to questions concerning the superiority, compatibility, complexity, cost, equity, and staff development of the TLM.

SUPERIORITY

Are this TLM and its accompanying strategies *superior* to instructional methods currently in place or to other methods that could be chosen?

COMPATIBILITY

Is this TLM *compatible* with the goals and aspirations of this school? Does this TLM match with other learning methods and strategies of the school?

COMPLEXITY

Is the *complexity* of the TLM, accompanying strategies, and equipment at a level that can be mastered by those who will be involved in using the learning method?

COST

Is this TLM *cost effective*? Could the same amount of money provide greater returns in student accomplishment if applied elsewhere?

EQUITY

Is this TLM *equitable* in the way it treats all groups within the student population: gender, racial, disabled, cultural, or socioeconomic ?

STAFF DEVELOPMENT

Is there, or will there be, sufficient *staff development* for those involved in the TLM to ensure its effective implementation in the classroom? Are both skills training and classroom applications addressed in the staff development plans for this TLM? Because of the critical nature of staff development for technology, Chapter 11 has been devoted to this issue.

PLANNED ABANDONMENT

Have plans been made for the *abandonment* of old teaching and learning practices that will be replaced by the TLM?

USING THE TAM THROUGH SIX STAGES

KEY QUESTION

How is the TAM used?

STAGE 1
Technology-Based Learning Method

Principals, with the appropriate members of the planning team, select a learning method that addresses the needs of their school building. A group of technology-wise administrators and teachers may need to blaze the trail in order to establish needs awareness on the part of the staff. The chosen TLM may be teacher-centered, an integrated learning system, electronic collaboration, hyperlearning, or electronic simulation.

STAGE 2
Front-End Analysis

In addition to the recurring decision elements, the principal and planning team seek to answer five questions in this stage of the TAM (review Figure 4).

1. Is there a *need* for this TLM?

2. Are there *users* on the staff who would profitably employ this TLM?

3. Is there *technology* sufficient to carry out this TLM?

4. Is the curriculum *content* amenable to this TLM?

5. Does this TLM suit the needs of the *students*?

STAGE 3
Classroom Testing

In addition to the recurring decision elements, the principal and planning team seek to answer four questions at this stage of the TAM.

1. Where can we find or create a classroom *demonstration* project for this TLM?

2. What *data* supports the installation of this TLM?

3. What have been the *subjective reviews* of this TLM?

4. Does this TLM enhance the building *curriculum*?

STAGE 4
Small-Scale Implementation

In addition to the recurring decision elements, the principal and planning team seek to answer five questions in this stage of the TAM.

1. What *modification* is necessary for further implementation of the TLM?

2. Has *data collection* supported the goals of this TLM?

3. What sort of *testing* adequately evaluates this TLM?

4. Is this TLM compatible with the overall *building goals*?

5. Is this TLM compatible with the *subject goals* in the applicable course of study?

STAGE 5
Districtwide Adoption

In addition to the recurring decision elements, the principal and planning team seek to answer five questions in this stage of the TAM.

1. Is the *hardware* available for districtwide installation of this TLM?

2. Can sufficient *training* for this TLM be assured?

3. Can adequate *support* for this TLM be assured?

4. Is there a long-term *commitment* for this TLM?

5. Is this TLM compatible with the *district mission*?

STAGE 6

Institutionalization

The final stage in this six-part flowchart focuses on three questions for effective institutionalization of a TLM.

1. Is sufficient, quality *staff development* planned to ensure the districtwide institutionalization of the chosen TLM?

2. Is sufficient *equipment* available to ensure the districtwide institutionalization of the chosen TLM?

3. Is sufficient *support* available to ensure the districtwide institutionalization of the chosen TLM?

Following the completion of the sixth stage of the TAM, the process begins again with investigation of a new TLM or the application of the same TLM to a different content area.

Recommended Readings for Chapter 10: Technology Adoption Model

Apple Computer, Inc. (1991). *Teaching, Learning & Technology: A planning guide.* Cupertino, CA: Apple Computer, Inc.

Bailey, G. D., and D. Lumley (1994). *Technology Staff Development Programs: A leadership sourcebook for school administrators.* New York: Scholastic.

Lumley, D., and G. D. Bailey (1993). *Planning for Technology: A guidebook for school administrators.* New York: Scholastic.

Center for Learning Technologies (1984). *Getting Started: Planning and implementing computer instruction in schools.* Albany, NY: Center for Learning Technologies.

Dede, C. (1989). Planning Guidelines for Emerging Instructional Technologies. *Educational Technology, 29*(4), 7–12.

Morehouse, D. E., and S. H. Stockdill (1992). Technology Adoption Model. *Educational Technology, 32*(2), 57–59.

CHAPTER 11

Professional Development

This chapter provides a brief survey for implementing a staff development program for technology-based learning. This chapter provides a four-stage model for technology staff development.

KEY QUESTIONS

What can principals and technology leaders do to effectively implement staff development for technology-based learning?

What kind of staff development program is necessary to successfully implement change in how teachers use the emerging technologies to engage students?

Staff development for technology is the crucial factor facing principals who want their staff to use technology-based learning methods (TLMs). A brief outline of strategies is provided in this chapter. This outline is not a substitute for a thorough, fully articulated and shared staff development program.

THE ROCKET OF STAFF DEVELOPMENT

An effective staff development program for technology depends on four factors occurring at the same place and the same time. These four factors—skills, resources, vision, and incentives—are much like the ingredients that combine in rocket engines to propel a spacecraft: They must all be brought together at the same time for an effective technology staff development program to take off. If any one factor is absent, takeoff is unlikely.

RESOURCES

Staff members learning to use technology progams and equipment in the classroom must have ready access to the equipment when they return to their regular stations from a staff development progam. Schools have often failed to provide equipment for teachers to practice and model effective technology use. If teachers are taught how to use equipment they will not have, they have no reason to learn the skill and no opportunity to practice it. Without such resources, the rocket of staff development lacks *fuel*.

SKILLS

Staff development leaders must be able to demonstrate the skills they are advocating. They must be able to walk the talk. They must have the ability to impart their skills to the participants of the staff development program. To talk about how to use technology without being able to demonstrate its use in the classroom is not sufficient. Without such skills, the rocket of staff development lacks *control*.

VISION

The leaders of the staff development program must have a clear vision of technology and technology's implications for the world and the classroom. Without such a vision, the rocket of staff development lacks *direction*.

INCENTIVES

Principals and staff development leaders must provide rewards and incentives for those involved in technology development. Teachers must know that their efforts are appreciated and supported by members of the administrative team and district governance. To ask staff members to embark on the difficult task of incorporating technology into new learning methods requires rewards. Without such incentives, the rocket of staff development lacks *riders*.

Outstanding principals and technology leaders are able to provide these four components in the right amounts at the right time. It is a complex skill—almost an art—to provide technology staff development and avoid the syndrome of "too much, too soon; too little, too late." Effective technology staff development for teachers brings the four factors of skills, resources, vision, and incentives together in an "on time, on target" program.

Finally, staff development for technology must be ongoing for the rocket to continue soaring. Withdraw any of the four factors and the rocket sputters and dies for a lack of propelling ingredients. Technology staff development is ongoing and continuous; it is not a one-shot deal. One-shot programs provide much noise and smoke, but the rocket crashes shortly after leaving the launchpad.

A FOUR-STAGE PLAN

A thorough treatment of staff development programs for integrating technology into education is found in *Technology Staff Development Programs—A Leadership Sourcebook for School Administrators* (1994) by Gerald Bailey and Dan Lumley. In this handbook, managing the complexity of a staff development program for implementing the various teaching methodologies is divided into four stages.

STAGE 1 : Prepare for change.

STAGE 2: Plan the program.

STAGE 3: Implement the program.

STAGE 4: Institutionalize the program.

The technology leader or principal can use these four stages to prepare the faculty for experimenting and exploring various technology-based learning methods.

STAGE 1
Prepare for Change

Instructional staff and other members involved in technology must understand the change process relative to emerging technologies. The change process requires having a vision. Technology leaders must have and provide skills, incentives, resources, and plans to implement the vision. Effective technology staff development programs prepare teachers for the change process and provide ownership in the vision for transforming schools.

In addition, teachers need to recognize that there are three different competencies found in professional development programs:

1. Knowledge—having an understanding of information

2. Attitudes—values or opinions related to the technology-based learning methods

3. Skills—specific behaviors that permit teachers to use emerging technologies to construct major learning methods

Teachers must also recognize that emerging technologies include a wide range of electronic technologies that are used to enhance teaching and learning. These include computer, interactive videodisc, CD-ROM, videotape, audiotape, television, facsimile transmission (fax), telephone, modem, robotics, virtual reality, etc.

Discussions focusing on these emerging technologies and how they can be used in creating various TLMs constitute the first stage of an effective technology staff development program. Essential to these discussions is the meaning of the terms *school reform*, *school restructuring*, and *school transformation* (see Preface).

STAGE 2
Plan the Program

Staff development is a key aspect of the technology adoption model in Chapter 10. Staff involvement in the design and implementation of technology programs is imperative. An effective technology staff development program creates leadership committees at both the district and building level to help craft the technology staff development program. The creation of two committees is important because both top-down and bottom-up staff development must occur. In essence, elements of the district technology staff development program need to ensure that district personnel, as well as building personnel, understand and are skilled at using the technology. Leadership must be exerted simultaneously at both levels for effective technology staff development programs.

The building principal is a key technology leader in the building technology staff development committee. The building leader as technology leader should exhibit a variety of technology leadership skills. The building leader, in crafting this program, should give careful consideration to involving key players impacted by the technology staff development program. These key players include the superintendent, school board members, parents, support staff, substitute teachers, and media/library specialists, as well as the primary users of the technology-based learning methods—the classroom teachers.

Careful use of audits can provide valuable information when planning technology staff development programs. The information gathered from the audits can be used to fashion guiding documents in the form of a mission statement, goals, and action plan. With a well-crafted plan in place, training in the technology-based learning methods can begin.

Without a written plan, technology staff development lacks direction. The written plan must identify the vision, skills, incentives, resources, and plan of action. With this in mind, implementation of technology staff development programs begins.

STAGE 3

Implement the Program

Specific elements of the TLM's training program should begin to explore the following concepts with regard to the technology-based methods:

- ◆ Teacher as guide on the side, mentor, co-learner, evaluator, and co-evaluator

- ◆ Basic literacy and information literacy (see Preface for a definition of information literacy)

Six basic principles should guide technology leaders as they consider how to deliver the technology staff development program.

1. No single delivery system is sufficient or correct in any one technology staff development program.

2. Technology-based learning methods need to be explored and used as participants are trained.

3. Most program gains and participant breakthroughs are made when people are allowed to work in teams.

4. Teams should be provided time to think, reflect, and dream.

5. Combining or offering alternative learning methods offers a more powerful learning environment than does relying exclusively on one TLM.

6. Participants usually have preferences of how to learn; therefore,

participants should have a choice in selecting one or more of the technology-based learning systems to learn about.

Activities

There are a variety of activities that should be considered.

1. Have teams brainstorm possible emerging technologies that could be used in TLMs.

2. Identify other schools or businesses that are using TLMs. Visit these locations, videotape, then allow committees to study and critique the TLMs in action.

3. Have teachers and administrators model one or more of the TLMs for others to watch, videotape, and critique.

4. Allow for and encourage a great deal of experimentation with the methodologies. Underscore the importance of experimentation without punishment or public embarrassment.

Learning Teams

The creation of learning teams as a major form of staff development is important. The learning cycle involved in mastering the TLMs should be considered in the training process. A training cycle includes four basic steps: 1) information, 2) demonstration, 3) practice, and 4) feedback and coaching.

STEP 1

Team members are exposed to and share information. A period of time is set aside to absorb new information and discuss the TLMs.

STEP 2

Team members schedule opportunities for watching one another demonstrate the TLMs.

STEP 3

Team members practice the behavior that has been previously discussed and observed. After practicing, team members can schedule a meeting to share their experiences and discuss their feelings and attitudes.

STEP 4

Team members ask for feedback and begin the coaching process. Coaching helps other team members master the skills required for the TLMs.

Critical Considerations

CONSIDER THE PHYSICAL ENVIRONMENT

The physical environment includes elements such as chairs, lighting, wall color, space, air flow, etc. The bottom line is that the physical environment must provide for those things that are going to be used back in the classroom.

CONSIDER INCENTIVES

Participants need a wide range of incentives.

CONSIDER CREATURE COMFORTS

Creature comforts can be defined as any food that is provided for participants or brought by participants. It has been said that armies march on their stomachs. If this is true, then staff developers are no different. Food and social interaction are natural and necessary in technology staff development programs.

CONSIDER PLUG-IN ENVIRONMENT AND HOT-LINE HELP

Participants need to feel that the equipment requires little preparation for use and that they have access to someone who can provide technical support. If overlooked, these two crucial elements portend difficulties for technology staff development programs (see Figure 5—Twenty Rules for Effective Technology Staff Development).

STAGE 4
Institutionalize the Program

The least-well-defined area of technology staff development is institutionalization. This process involves evaluation of the technology-based learning methods. They must be scrutinized for refinement or abandonment. Questions arising from the technology adoption model (TAM) in Chapter 10, such as effectiveness, cost, compatibility, complexity, equity, abandonment, and modification, must be asked by technology staff development committees.

As these decisions are made, public relations becomes a central strategy for institutionalizing TLMs. Public relations strategies for promoting the TLMs include:

1. Making presentations to civic and social organizations

2. Sending memos to major constituencies

3. Placing notices on bulletin boards—both traditional and electronic

4. Sending out newsletters

Figure 5

Twenty Rules for Technology Staff Development Activities

1. Participants must physically take part in activities—hands-on.

2. Participants must acquire classroom skills.

3. Participants must receive rewards (money, time, recognition).

4. Participants must be volunteers.

5. Participants must produce something.

6. Participants must include building and district administrators.

7. Activities must have the three parts of the Joyce and Showers model: theory, practice, coaching.

8. Activities must be related to perceived needs.

9. Activities must develop a concept.

10. Activities must include a plan of action.

11. Activities must include an opportunity for follow-up practice.

12. Activities must address creature comforts.

13. Activities must include shared learning with colleagues.

14. Activities must take place in a training facility for adults.

15. Activities must be fun.

16. Activities must take people from where they are.

17. Activities must address multiple intelligences and learning styles.

18. "Hot-line" help is a must.

19. Teachers must work in a "one-plug" or "one-switch" environment.

20. The technology must be present in the classroom.

FIGURE 5: Twenty Rules for Technology Staff Development Activities

5. Providing articles, newsletters, updates, and status reports on new directions of the projects

6. Using cable TV to highlight achievements

SUMMARY

A well-defined technology staff development program must be in place to support the TLMs. The technology staff development program takes considerable thought and cannot be implemented without a comprehensive plan. Once in place, the TLMs have the potential to transform the learning process and create learners for the twenty-first century.

Recommended Readings for Chapter 11: Staff Development

Bailey, G. D., and G. Bailey (1994). *101 Activities for Creating Effective Technology Staff Development Programs: A sourcebook of games, stories, role playing and learning exercises for administrators.* New York: Scholastic.

Bailey, G. D., and D. Lumley (1994). *Technology Staff Development Programs: A leadership sourcebook for administrators.* New York: Scholastic.

Costa, A. (1991). Staff Developers: Tinkerers or transformers: Nine perspectives on the future of staff developement. *Journal of Staff Development, 12*(1), 5–6.

Fullan, M. G., and S. Stiegelbauer (1991) *The New Meaning of Educational Change.* New York: Teacher's College.

Hort, S. M. (1992). *Facilitative Leadership: The imperative for change.* Austin, TX: Southwest Educational Development Laboratory.

Joyce, B., and B. Showers (1988). *Student Achievement Through Staff Development.* New York: Longman.

Marshall, G. (1988). Computer Training for Teachers Must Be Practical and Relevant. *Executive Educator, 10*(3), 26–27.

November, A. (1993). Risky Business: Redefining professional development. *Electronic Learning, 12*(5), 16.

Schlechty, P. C. (1993). On the Frontier of School Reform with Trailblazers, Pioneers and Settlers. *Journal of Staff Development, 14*(4), 46–51.

Venditti, P. N. (1994). From Hermit to Helper: A taxonomy of technological experts in education. *Educational Technology, 34*(6), 48–50.

PART IV

Resources for Technology Adoption by Principals

Glossary

*The following definitions may help
building principals become
familiar with the terms used in
restructuring with technology.*

Analog: Analog signals are stored as a continuous, smooth wave that mimics the waves of the original sound (Apple Computer, Inc., 1991). Unfortunately, the quality of analog signals deteriorates over time. Each time a sound is copied, it loses some fidelity, and when transmitted, it picks up extraneous noise (U. S. Congress, Office of Technology Assessment, 1988).

Animation: The imitation of movement produced by showing a series of images on the screen (Microsoft, 1991).

ASCII (text) files: An ASCII (American Standard for Code Information Interchange) file is one that is composed entirely of characters that can by typed from a keyboard. It contains no graphics or special codes for printing (Jordahl, 1991). ASCII assigns a numeric value to letters (Microsoft, 1991).

Audiographic systems: Systems that use computers as interactive electronic chalkboards and for two-way audio conferencing (Whisler, 1988).

Audio teleconferencing: A distance technology that uses telephones and speakerphones to allow more than one person to speak or listen (Whisler, 1988).

Backbone: A central network that connects several others, usually lower-bandwidth networks or computing devices, so that they can communicate electronically with each other (Ohlson and Michael, 1992).

Backup: A copy of a program, disc, or document made to ensure the safety of the original against loss (Microsoft, 1991).

Bandwidth: The information-carrying capacity of a communications system, generally measured in bits per second (Ohlson and Michael, 1992).

Baseband network: A type of local area network such as ethernet or AppleTalk. This type of networking limits the speed of transmission and distance separating machines (Microsoft, 1991).

Battery backup: A battery-operated supply used as an alternative source of power in the event of electrical failure (Microsoft, 1991).

Baud/bits per second (bps): Both refer to the rate of speed at which information is transferred via modem over a phone connection (Jordahl, 1991).

Bells and whistles: A jargon term used to describe extra features added to hardware or software that are unnnecessary for basic operation (Microsoft, 1991).

Binary files: Those files containing information not represented in the file by ASCII characters. These may be graphics, formatted files, or even programs (Jordahl, 1991).

BITNET (Because It's Time Network): The U.S. network linking colleges, universities, and research institutions (Jordahl, 1991).

Boolean: A type of mathematical expression having to do with true-false values rather than numerical calculations. Many computer operations rely on the Boolean logical operators *and*, *or*, and *not* (Microsoft, 1991).

Broadband network: A type of local area network on which transmissions travel as radio frequencies on separate channels. It can handle significantly higher rates of transmission over greater distances than baseband (Microsoft, 1991).

Bulletin board system (BBS): An area within a network where users "post" information for public display (Jordahl, 1991).

Bus network: A topology for a local area network in which all devices are connected to a main line of communication (Microsoft, 1991).

Cathode-ray tube (CRT): The basis of television screens and standard microcomputer screens (Microsoft, 1991).

Clip art: A collection of photographs, diagrams, maps, drawings, and graphics that can be "clipped" from the collection and incorporated into documents (Microsoft, 1991).

Coaxial cable: An electrical cable consisting of a wire surrounded by a cylindrical conductor, which has the same axis (Ohlson and Michael, 1992).

Collaborative learning: When a group sets out to discover or create an understanding of a significant phenomenon. Collaboration is a purposive relationship created to solve a problem or discover something (Schrage, 1990).

Compact disc-audio (CD-Audio): Sound interactively accessed by a computer from ordinary compact discs such as those on sale in record stores (Apple Computer, Inc., 1991).

Compact disc-interactive (CD-I): A hardware and software standard for optical disc technology that combines audio, video, and text on high-capacity compact discs (Microsoft, 1991).

Compact disc read-only memory (CD-ROM): A variant of audio compact disc that stores extremely large amounts of data—including text, graphics, animation, sound, and video—for future use by a computer (Apple Computer, Inc., 1991). CD-ROM drives are separate from discs. As the discs are relatively cheap and have a large storage capacity, they are appropriate for distribution of multimedia. They cannot be modified by the user.

Computer-aided design/computer-aided manufacturing (CAD/CAM): The process in which a computer is used to develop scale drawings of a product that is later produced by computer-assisted technology.

Computer literacy: Knowledge and an understanding of computers combined with the ability to use them effectively (Microsoft, 1991).

Conferencing: A term used to indicate when several network users communicate on a particular subject (Jordahl, 1991).

Connect-time charges: The fees network information sources charge users for the time they spend on-line (Jordahl, 1991).

Constructivist psychology: Learners construct and then reconstruct mental models that organize ideas and their interrelationships (Shepard, 1991).

Cooperative learning: Robert Slavin's (1983) model is based on specific group rewards for team members' learning and task specialization. Asks students to work together to solve problems, locate information, and make presentations (Bruce, 1992).

Cyberspace: Another term for virtual reality, where users are immersed in a computer-generated, three-dimensional world (Lantz, 1992).

Daisy chain: A set of devices connected one after another along a single line (Microsoft, 1991).

Database: Loosely, any aggregation of data; a file consisting of a number of records, each of which is constructed of fields of a particular type, together with a collection of operations that facilitate searching, sorting, and combining activities (Microsoft, 1991).

DB connector: Any of several types of cable ends used to connect serial and parallel input and output ports of computer equipment (Microsoft, 1991).

Desktop publishing: The use of computers and specialized software to combine text and graphics to create documents ready for publication (Microsoft, 1991).

Digital: Refers to signals that have been converted into a series of discrete numerical values. In playback, these numeric values are reproduced exactly, without the distortion that inevitably creeps into older analog methods (Lynch, Apple Corp., 1991; U. S. Congress, Office of Technology Assessment, 1988).

Digital video-interactive (DV-I): A hardware/software system that uses compression of digital video and audio for use in microcomputer applications (Microsoft, 1991).

Digitized audio: Allows instructors to incorporate unique audio materials into teaching applications. With audio digitization, any sounds or music from a tape, record, CD, or live recording can be captured for use in multimedia teaching projects (Apple Computer, Inc., 1991).

Disk: A round, flat piece of flexible plastic (floppy) or inflexible metal (hard disk) coated with a magnetic material used to store information in digital form (Microsoft, 1991).

Distance learning: The use of telecommunications devices—such as satellite, television, fiber optics, telephone, or fax machine—to send instructional programming to learners (Rockman and Lillenthal, 1992).

Distributed network: Computers are placed in individual classrooms rather than in a networked computer lab.

Electronic mail (E-Mail): A computer "mailbox" where users receive and send personal letters, belong to public forums, and exchange information with other attached users over electronic connections (Eiser, 1990).

Ergometrics: The study of people vis-a-vis their working environment (Microsoft, 1991).

Ethernet: A local area network using a bus topography providing baseband transmission at 10 megabytes per second (Microsoft, 1991).

Ethernet cable: Cable that meets the specifications for the type of cable that can be use on an ethernet network (thick or thin coaxial or twisted pair) (Ohlson and Michael, 1992).

Fax: A technology used to send documents over phone lines. Text and graphics are reduced to digital form and transmitted to distant locations (Microsoft, 1991). Facsimile machines reduce documents to digital signals, transmit these signals over ordinary phone lines, and reproduce copies at distant locations.

Fiber-optic: Wire that carries an electrical signal that has been converted to light signals at high speeds across great distance with little distortion (Lipson, 1992). Cabling is sometimes referred to as glass—glass filament conducts pulses converted from electrical signals.

File server: A storage device on a network that is accessible to all users of the network (Microsoft, 1991).

File-transfer protocols: The method by which files are transferred to or from a host computer. Usually refers to error-correcting procedures that check for problems during transfer and resend incorrect data (Pettacia, 1993).

Floppy disk: A round, flat piece of coated plastic encased in a plastic cover and used to store information (Microsoft, 1991). Floppy disks are low-capacity, fast-access magnetic storage. They can be used to store text, sound, or graphics, but their low capacity limits their utility in multimedia applications (Kaplan-Neher, 1989).

Flowchart: Shows the path data takes through a program (Microsoft, 1991).

Footprint: The surface area a personal computer or peripheral occupies on a desktop (Microsoft, 1991).

Freeware: Free computer programs (Microsoft, 1991).

Freeze-frame video: An electronic slide show transmitted by video. An instructor uses a video camera focused on a printer, graphic materials, blackboard, or people to capture an image for transmission over a phone line (Whisler, 1988).

Garbage in, garbage out (GIGO): Computer jargon referring to the nonthinking nature of a computer and its processes (Microsoft, 1991).

Gateway: A device or program connecting two LANs using different protocols, translating these protocols are devices on these two networks that enable them to communicate with each other (Ohlson and Michael, 1992).

Gigabyte: 1 billion bytes.

Graphical user interface (GUI): A display format that allows users to choose commands, start programs, and see lists of files and other options by pointing to pictorial representations (icons) and lists of menu items on the screen (Microsoft, 1991).

Groupware: A collective term for software that allows users to collaborate gracefully over time and distance (Johnson, 1991).

Guide: A commercial software product of Owl Inc. that allows authors to use electronic hypertext.

Handshake: A signal acknowledging that communications can take place; usually involves modems and telecommunications (Microsoft, 1991).

Hard disk: Mass storage devices having a higher storage capacity than floppy disks and faster access than optical storage systems (Syllabus, 1989).

Hayes-compatible: Modems that respond to the same set of commands as a modem manufactured by Hayes Microcomputer Products. The de facto standard for microcomputer modems (Microsoft, 1991).

High-definition television (HDTV): Any production or delivery mechanism designed to display images in real time with 1,000 lines of resolution or more (McKinney, 1991).

Hologram: A three-dimensional figure created by holography (Microsoft, 1991).

Hub: A device that extends the maximum physical length of a network by clearing and retransmitting signals among network segments (Ohlson and Michael, 1992).

HyperCard: A commercial software product of Claris Corporation that allows authors to use electronic hypertext. It has been described as an electronic stack of index cards (Apple Computer, Inc., 1989; Minnesota State Department of Education, 1990a).

Hypermedia: Hypertextual documents containing text, graphics, animation, sound, or motion video.

Hypertext: Chunks of textual information connected associatively (Jonassen, 1989).

Icon: A small graphical user interface (GUI) image displayed on the screen to represent an object that can be manipulated by the user (Microsoft, 1991).

Instruction by satellite: Usually involves a program from a broadcast studio in which student and teacher can hear and respond to each other. Some include computer-assisted instruction components; some do not (Whisler, 1988).

Internet: An electronic mail system connecting governmental institutions, military branches, educational institutions, and commercial companies (Jordahl, 1991).

Kermit: A telecommunications protocol used mostly by educational institutions and older mainframes. The slowest of all protocols (Pettacia, 1993).

Links: The relations that connect nodes of information in a program such as Linkway® or HyperCard® (Marchionini, 1988).

Linkway®: An IBM software package that performs similar functions to Claris HyperCard®.

Liquid crystal display (LCD): A type of display that uses a liquid compound to display data (Microsoft, 1991).

Local area networks (LAN): The smallest of networking topologies, usually covering areas of less than two miles (Motorola Codex, 1992). They often link computers in one building to nearby buildings (Maddux and Willis, 1992). Local Area Network is a group of connected, intercommunicating computers that share peripheral devices residing within a limited geographic area (Ohlson and Michael, 1992).

Log-off: The sequence of events that occurs when the caller disconnects from the host system.

Log-on: The sequence of events that occurs when the caller connects to the host system.

Mainframe: A high-level, expensive computer, designed for intensive computations tasks. Because of its complexity and expense, it is often shared by multiple users (Microsoft, 1991).

Modem: The boxlike device that connects a computer to a phone line and allows data to be transmitted (Jordahl, 1991).

Multimedia: Application or utilities programs that integrate text, sound, graphics, still images, animation, and video for computer-generated presentations (Gill, 1992). Sometimes a subset of hypermedia (Microsoft, 1991).

Musical Instrument Digital Interface (MIDI): The standard way for both professional and amateur musicians to connect synthesizers, keyboards, and other musical instruments to computers (Bove and Rhodes, 1990).

National Television Standards Committee (NTSC): The organization that established the standard for television production and broadcast. It set the current 525-scanning-line-per-frame standard in the U.S. (McKinney, 1991).

Network: A group of computers and peripheral devices, such as printers, that are interconnected so that they can communicate with each other (Ohlson and Michael, 1992).

Nodes: The informational units of hypertext: paragraphs, images, articles, lessons, etc. (Marchionini, 1988).

Platform: The basic technology of a computer system. The most common platforms are Apple and IBM (Microsoft, 1991).

Plotter: Any device used to draw charts, diagrams, and other graphics similar to the work done by draftspersons (Microsoft, 1991).

Power user: A person skilled with computers (Microsoft, 1991).

Public-domain software: A program donated for public use by its owner (Microsoft, 1991).

Red-green-blue (RGB): A mixing model used with many color monitors (Microsoft, 1991).

Ring network: A local area network topology in which devices are connected in a closed loop or ring as opposed to a bus network (Microsoft, 1991).

Second-person: A virtual-reality system that uses a video camera as an input device. Users see images on a large video monitor or video project image, which the computer processes to include extra features such as movements, positions, and number of fingers raised.

Server (or file server): A microcomputer with a large hard drive. It contains the ILS management system, ILS courseware, and student records. It may also contain third-party software (Mageau, 1992).

Simulation: Electronic substitutes for actual experience.

Single in-line memory module (SIMM): Device used to add memory to computers (Microsoft, 1991).

Small computer system interface (SCSI): A parallel cabling scheme for connecting peripheral devices such as CD-ROM and color scanners (Microsoft, 1991).

Spell checker: An application program that checks for misspellings in documents.

Spreadsheet program: An application commonly used for finance-related tasks (Microsoft, 1991).

Star network: A network scheme in which devices are connected to a central computer in a star-shaped topology as opposed to a bus topology (Microsoft, 1991).

Telepublishing: The process of transmitting pages of text and graphics via telecommunications for display on a monitor and reproduction (Mulvey, 1991).

Terminal emulation: The ability of the telecommunications software package to imitate a type of computer the host requires. Common settings are TTY and VT100 (Pettacia, 1993).

Thicknet: This cable can support longer distances than thinnet (500 meters) and can have up to 100 nodes connected to it (Lipson, 1992).

Thinnet: This cable looks similar to television cable and is often used to connect networks within limited distances (185 meters) and limited nodes (35) (Lipson, 1992).

Token-ring: A networked ring of devices that passes a special bit pattern, called a token, from node to node, deciding which device can transmit data on the network (Ohlson and Michael, 1992).

Total immersion: Virtual-reality systems designed to produce a feeling of complete immersion in the environment by using wide-angle stereoscopic head-mounted displays, simulated three-dimensional audio, and a remote handheld (or glove) manipulator (Lantz, 1992).

Turnkey: An ILS installation in which the vendor is responsible for installation of the entire system: hardware, wiring, software, and management.

Twisted-pair: The type of cable commonly associated with connecting phone-line devices (Lipson, 1992).

Two-way interactive television: Real-time two-way visual contact between an instructor and students, generally incorporating an interactive audio component (Whisler, 1988).

Upload/download: Sending information over a network/receiving information over a network (Jordahl, 1991).

Videodisc: A plastic platter that has digitally encoded information in a wide variety of instructional formats: slides, filmstrips, motion pictures, charts, graphs, data, dual audio, illustrations, microfilm, videotape, and text (Minnesota State Department of Education, 1991).

Web learning: Knowledge acquisition that can be seen as a series of developing structures that are tested, modified, or replaced in ways that facilitate learning and thinking (Shepard, 1991).

Wide area networks (WAN): A networking topology with national and international spans (Motorola Codex, 1992). A group of computer devices connected over long distance, often by telephone lines or satellite transmission (Ohlson and Michael, 1992).

Word processor: An application program for manipulating text-based documents; the electronic equivalent of paper, pen, typewriter, eraser, and most likely dictionary and thesaurus (Microsoft, 1991).

Write once, read many (WORM) disks: An optical storage medium. Currently, WORM drives' access time is slow, but they can store large amounts of information (Kaplan-Neher, 1989).

Virtual reality: A highly interactive, computer-based multimedia environment that enables users to participate directly in real-time, three-dimensional environments generated by computers (Helsel, 1992, 1991).

XMODEM: The most common error-checking protocol for use in modem transmissions over phone lines. (Pettacia, 1993).

YMODEM: An error-checking protocol for modem transmissions. Ymodem is faster than XMODEM (Pettacia, 1993).

ZMODEM: The fastest error-checking protocol of modem transmissions (Pettacia, 1993).

APPENDIX B

Vendors

This appendix contains ten vendors that have been selected as representative of a growing field of software and hardware suppliers. There are no more that ten vendors for each of the five learning methods. Because the technology and the vendors of educational technology are changing so rapidly, principals wishing to implement technology-based learning methods should pay particular attention to vendor listings in trade magazines such as MacWorld, MacUser, PC World, PC User, *and professional magazines such as* T.H.E. Journal, Electronic Learning, *and* Curriculum Product News. *There are literally thousands of firms providing products for electronic learning methods.*

TEACHER-CENTERED LEARNING WITH TECHNOLOGY

Apple Computer, Inc.
20525 Mariani Ave.
Cupertino, CA 95014
(800) 776-2333

Beagle Brothers
6215 Ferris Square
San Diego, CA 92121
(619) 452-5500

EduQuest (IBM)
P. O. Box 2150
Atlanta, GA 30055
(800) 426-3327

Focus Enhancements
800 W. Cummings Park, Suite 4500
Woburn, MA 01801
(800) 538-8866

Hewlett-Packard
P. O. Box 58059
Santa Clara, CA 95051
(800) 752-0900

Microsoft Corporation
1 Microsoft Way
Redmond, WA 98052
(800) 426-9400

Scholastic Software
730 Broadway
New York, NY 10003
(800) 541-5513

Texas Instruments, Inc.
5701 Airport Rd.
Temple, TX 76503
(800) 527-3500

TI-IN
1000 Central Parkway North
San Antonio, TX 78232
(800) 999-8446

Tom Snyder
80 Coolidge Hill Rd.
Watertown, MA 02172-2817
(800) 342-2817

INTEGRATED LEARNING SYSTEMS

Computer Curriculum Corporation
1287 Lawrence State Rd.
Sunnyvale, CA 94088
(800) 227-8324

Computer Networking Specialists
61 E. Main St., P. O. Box 2075
Walla Walla, WA 99362
(800) 372-3277

Computer Systems Research
Avon Park South, P. O. Box 45
Avon, CT 06001
(800) 922-1190

Ideal Learning Systems
8505 Freeport Pkwy., Suite 360
Irving, TX 75063
(800) 999-3234

Josten's Learning Corporation
6170 Cornerstone Court East
San Diego, CA 92121
(800) 521-8538

New Century Education
220 Old New Brunswick Rd.
Melville, NY 11747
(800) 526-4566

TRO/PLATO
4660 W. 77th St.
Edina, MN 55435
(800) 869-2000

Wasatch Education Systems
5250 South 300 West, Suite 350
Salt Lake City, UT 84107
(800) 877-2848

WICAT Education
1875 South State St.
Orem, UT 85048
(800) 759-4228

ELECTRONIC COLLABORATIVE LEARNING

Applied Engineering
3210 Beltline Rd.
Dallas, TX 75234
(800) 554-6227

Asante Technologies
404 Tasman
Sunnyvale, CA 94089
(800) 662-9686

AT&T Network Systems
475 South St.
Morristown, NJ 07962
(800) 344-0223

CC: Mail
2141 Landing's Dr.
Mountain View, CA 94043
(800) 448-2500

CE Software
1801 Industrial Circle, P. O. Box 65580
West Des Moines, IA 50265
(800) 523-7638

Dove Corporation
1200 N. 23rd. St.
Wilmington, NC 28405
(800) 849-3297

Farallon Computing
2000 Powell St., Suite 600
Emeryville, CA 94608
(510) 596-9000

Global Village Communications
685 E. Middlefield Rd., Bldg. B
Mountain View, CA 94043
(800) 736-4821

Novell, Inc.
122 E. 1700 St.
Provo, UT 84606
(800) 453-1267

Shiva Corporation
One Cambridge Center
Cambridge, MA 02142
(800) 458-3550

HYPERLEARNING

Authorware Inc.
275 Shoreline Dr., Suite 535
Redwood City, CA 94065
(800) 288-9576

Claris Corporation
5201 Patrick Henry Dr.
Santa Clara, CA 95052
(408) 727-8227

IBM Corporation
P.O. Box 2150
Atlanta, GA
(800) 426-2468

Intellimation
130 Cremona Dr., P. O. Box 1922
Santa Barbara, CA 93116
(800) 346-8355

Macromedia
600 Townsend St.
San Francisco, CA 94103
(415) 442-0200

SuperMac Technology
485 Potreto Ave.
Sunnyvale, CA 94086
(800) 334-3005

Voyager Company
1351 Pacific Coast Highway
Santa Monica, CA 90401
(800) 446-2001

Sony Corporation of America
MD-3-17 Sony Dr.
Park Ridge, NJ 07656
(201) 930-6177

Teaching Technologies
P. O. Box 3808
San Luis Obispo, CA 93403-3808
(805) 541-3100

Wings for Learning
1600 Green Hills Rd.
P.O. Box 660002
Scotts Valley, CA 95067
(800) 321-7511

Wolfram Research, Inc.
100 Trade Center Dr.
Champaign, IL 61820
(800) 451-5151

ELECTRONIC LEARNING SIMULATIONS

Autodesk
2320 Marinship Way
Sausalito, CA 94965
(415) 332-2344

Broderbund Software, Inc.
500 Redwood Blvd.
Novato, CA 94948
(800) 521-6263

Knowledge Revolution
15 Brush Place
San Francisco, CA 94103
(415) 553-8153

MECC
6160 Summit Dr. North
Minneapolis, MN 55430
(800) 685-6322

Transparencies

This section contains transparency masters that correspond to technology-based learning methods (TLMs) of the technology adoption model. Although they may be used with any part of the handbook, they have been grouped to match specific TLMs. These transparencies may prove useful when making presentations to teachers, parents, and other stakeholders.

TEACHING _WITH_ TECHNOLOGY

**Effective Schools
and Technology**

*

**Technology as an
Educational Tool**

TEACHING _WITH_ TECHNOLOGY

Some Instructional Strategies:

Computer Drill and Practice

*

Lecture with an LCD Panel

*

Videotape Presentation

*

Interactive TV Lessons

*

Multimedia Presentation

TEACHING
ABOUT
TECHNOLOGY

Some Examples:

Willard Daggett

*

SCANS Report

*

Technology Preparation Programs

*

Technology Education Programs

TEACHING _ABOUT_ TECHNOLOGY

Some Instructional Strategies:

Build an Airplane
Build a Bridge

*

Statistical Control

*

Computer-Assisted Design
and Manufacturing

EMPOWERING
WITH
TECHNOLOGY

Some Examples:

Robert Reich:
Symbolic Analyst

*

Marshall McLuhan:
Suspended Judgment

*

Seymour Papert:
Technology-Infused
Environments

EMPOWERING
WITH
TECHNOLOGY

Some Learning Strategies:

Anyone, Learning
Anything,
Anytime,
Anywhere

*

Mastering
Technology-Infused
Environments

*

Information Literacy

Southwestern Kansas

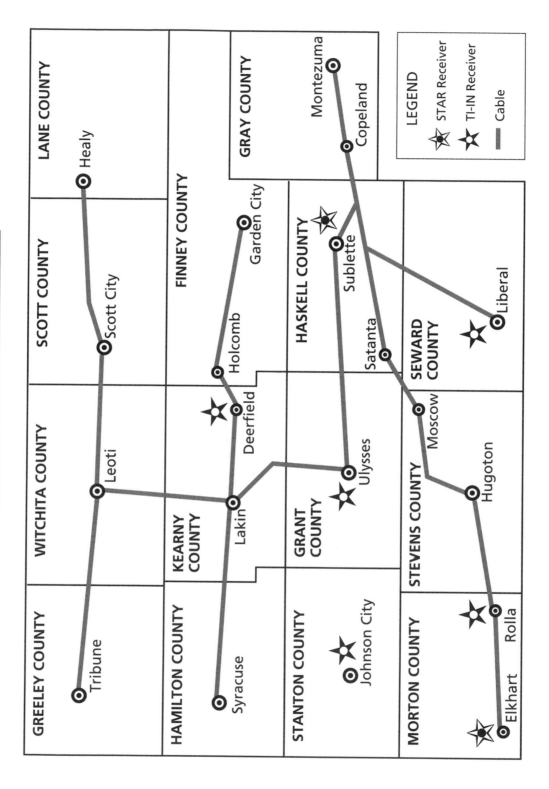

SMART BUYING TACTICS FOR TECHNOLOGY

Performance

*

Cost

*

Expandability

*

Service and Support

*

Design and Construction

MAKING YOUR ILS A SUCCESS

Principal = ILS Leader

*

Help Teachers Fit ILS into Curriculum

*

Provide Incentives for Teachers

*

Give Teachers Time to Preview Lessons

*

Hire a Competent ILS System Manager

*

Use the Reports

*

Have Curriculum-Correlation
Charts Handy

Sample Collaborative Classroom

Communications Medium and Bandwidth

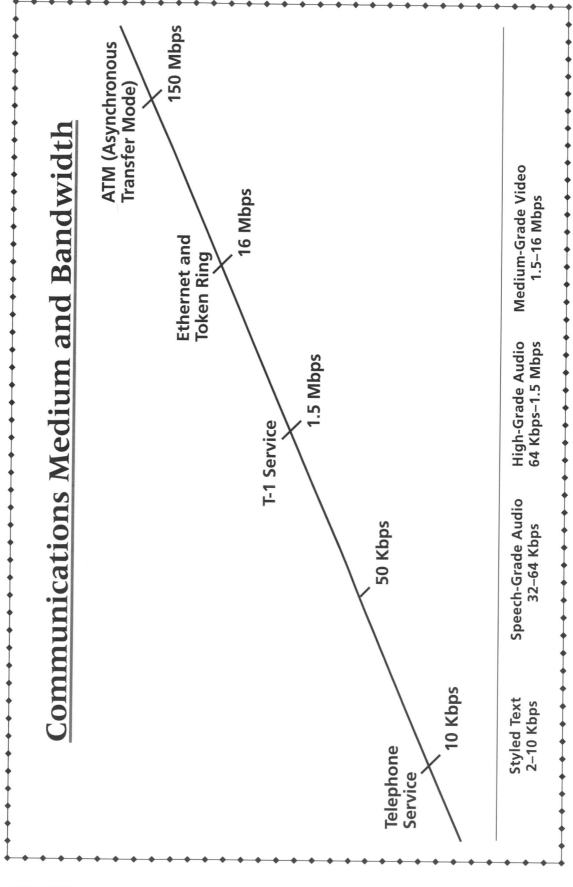

ATM (Asynchronous Transfer Mode) — 150 Mbps

Ethernet and Token Ring — 16 Mbps

T-1 Service — 1.5 Mbps

50 Kbps

Telephone Service — 10 Kbps

Styled Text
2–10 Kbps

Speech-Grade Audio
32–64 Kbps

High-Grade Audio
64 Kbps–1.5 Mbps

Medium-Grade Video
1.5–16 Mbps

Star Topology

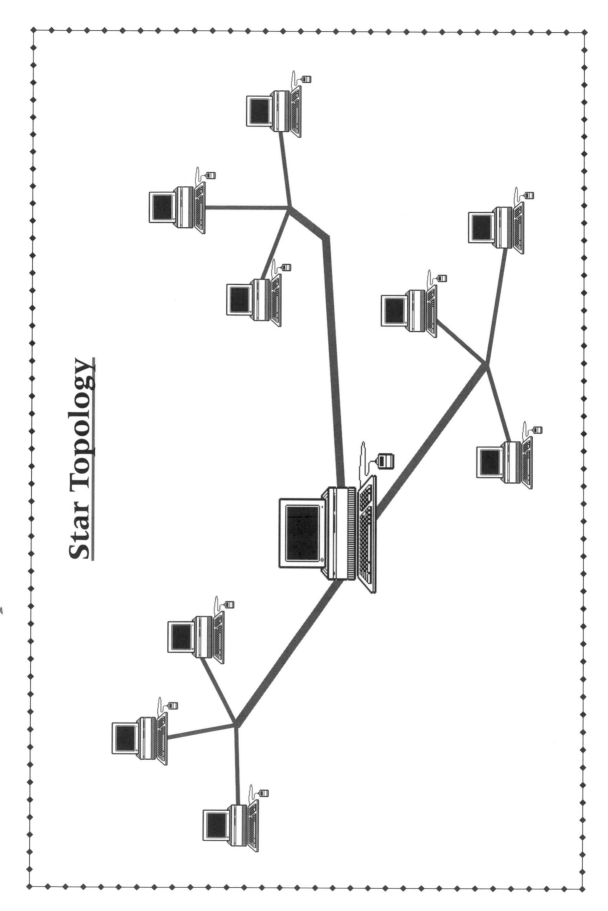

Bus Topology

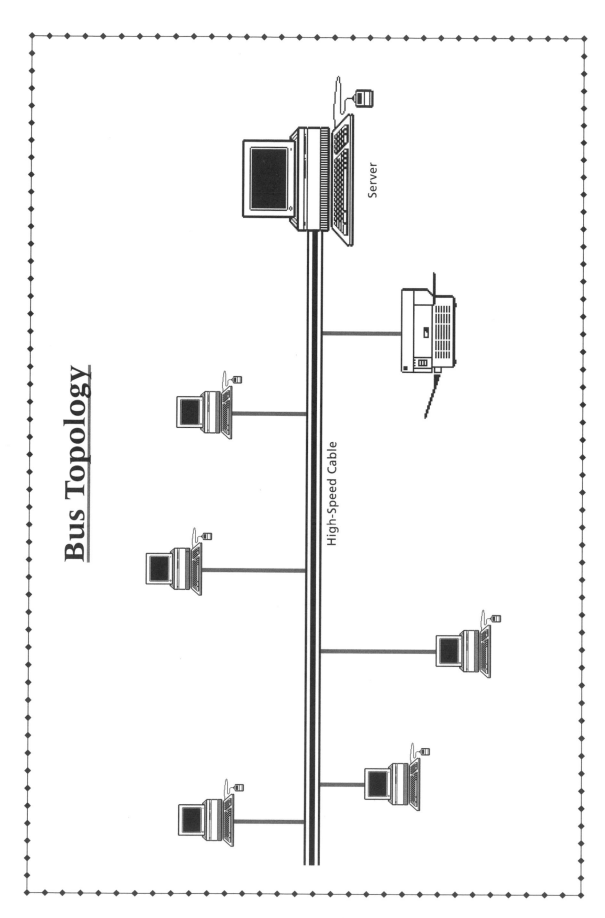

Server

High-Speed Cable

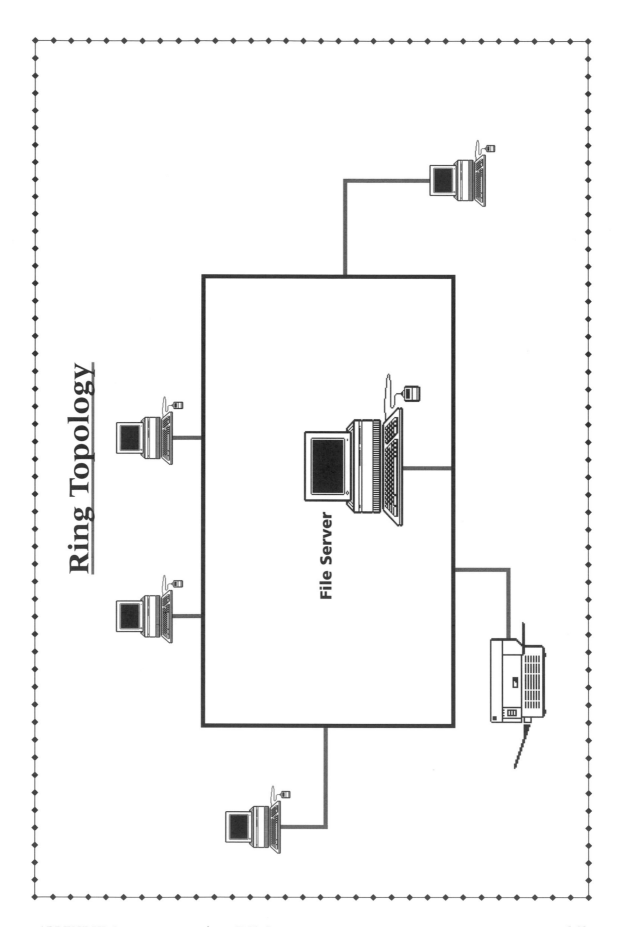

Ring Topology

File Server

Checklists

The following checklists are designed to help building principals ensure that fundamental issues have been addressed when implementing a technology-based learning method (TLM). The first checklist highlights the recurring decision elements of the technology adoption model. The following five checklists are specific to a chosen TLM in the handbook. These checklists have been produced in a size that allows them to be used as transparencies. The checklists can be used for discussion with major stakeholders in the implementation process, and as review for teachers and principals establishing a TLM.

RECURRING DECISION ELEMENTS
TECHNOLOGY ADOPTION MODEL

_____ **Superiority:** Using this technology provides superior instruction to the students.

_____ **Compatibility:** Software or hardware match with the already installed technology base and curriculum program.

_____ **Cost:** Significant costs have been anticipated. This is a cost-effective way of providing for or improving student learning.

_____ **Complexity:** The equipment or software is within reach of the people who will be using it.

_____ **Equity:** Equipment and software effectively meet the needs of all student groups: gender, racial, disabled, and socioeconomic.

_____ **Staff Development:** Sufficient technical and developmental training is provided to ensure effectiveness of this chosen method.

_____ **Planned Abandonment:** Plans have been made for abandoning teaching practices that are outdated or replaced by technology-based learning methods.

TEACHER-CENTERED LEARNING WITH TECHNOLOGY

_____ **Expandability:** Software or equipment can be expanded and developed to provide greater service to the educational process.

_____ **Curriculum:** Clearly defined curriculum purposes aligned with already installed objectives have been identified.

_____ **Sufficiency:** This technology is complete by itself or as part of a larger project.

_____ **Evaluation:** Evaluation of teachers using this technology adequately reflects new teaching styles using emerging technologies.

_____ **Assessment:** Student assessment includes methods for measuring student learning from emerging technology instruction.

_____ **Hot-Line Help:** Prompt support is available to help teachers using technology solve minor technical difficulties.

_____ **Time:** Time periods for distance learning opportunities have been accommodated.

_____ **Cart:** The cart chosen for teacher use of technological equipment:

- ◆ Is sturdy
- ◆ Has large wheels
- ◆ Can access all classrooms
- ◆ Plugs and plays, and
- ◆ Is assigned to an individual for support and scheduling

_____ **Software Selection:** Software selection procedures that ensure for teacher and community input have been established.

_____ **Distance Learning:** Staff concerns for distance learning have been addressed. Specifically they are:

- ◆ Certification of teachers
- ◆ Negotiated agreements
- ◆ Responsibilities of the local district
- ◆ Time and place of delivery

_____ **Security:** Procedures for protecting the hardware and software from theft, vandalism, and unauthorized duplications have been established.

_____ **Electricity:** Classrooms have adequate electrical outlets to operate the equipment without unsightly and dangerous extension cords.

_____ **Lighting:** Classroom lighting can be controlled by the teacher for maximum effectiveness of the technology.

INTEGRATED LEARNING SYSTEMS

_____ **Expandability:** Software or equipment can be expanded and developed to provide greater service to the educational process.

_____ **Curriculum:** Clearly defined curriculum purposes aligned with already installed objectives have been identified.

_____ **Curriculum Guides:** Curriculum guides that match the ILS with the classroom curriculum have been prepared for all teachers.

_____ **Training:** Plans for required training of both teachers and lab monitors are in place.

_____ **Licensing Agreements:** Clearly spelled out ownerships, upgrade renewals, and maintenance of the instructional and managerial software are in place.

_____ **Lab vs. Classroom Placement:** Placement of the ILS has been decided and planned for, including both room and staff development.

_____ **Facility:** Placement and facility considerations have been addressed for comfort, safety, and security.

_____ **Management and Reporting:** Effective use of the management and reporting capabilities of the ILS has been planned for to include parent communication and student educational programming modification.

_____ **Software Selection:** Software selection procedures have been established that ensure for teacher and community input.

ELECTRONIC COLLABORATIVE LEARNING

_____ **Collaboration:** Collaborative and cooperative learning models are understood and in place.

_____ **Roles:** Roles are clearly assigned within the collaborative learning model, even though distance and time are involved.

_____ **Literacy:** Information literacy is an applied concept, with students and faculty able to electronically search and communicate over time and distance.

_____ **Time:** Different class times and time zones have been anticipated.

_____ **Security:** Security of the network from a variety of threats has been planned for during the installation phase of an electronic network. These threats include viruses, unauthorized access, and software piracy.

_____ **Communicative Compatibility:** Communication devices at all locations are compatible and use the same protocols for effective networking.

_____ **Staff Development:** Staff development for the multiple computer skills required for technology-based cooperative learning have been put in place.

HYPERLEARNING

_____ **Assessment:** Designs for assessment of student-centered learning are in place and have been clearly communicated to students, parents, and teachers.

_____ **Cognitive Overload:** The dangers of swamping students in a sea of knowledge have been addressed.

_____ **Search Strategies:** Students have acquired adequate search strategies and tactics for the level of student-centered learning expected.

_____ **Navigation:** Navigation standards have been established at the beginning to prevent students from becoming lost in hyperlearning environments. Plans for a balance between control and unbridled wandering have been established.

_____ **Web and Constructionist Theories of Learning:** Staff development for these theories of learning are in place.

ELECTRONIC LEARNING SIMULATIONS

_____ **Gaming:** Safeguards have been installed to ensure that the simulation matches the curriculum and that students do not play games with little educational merit.

_____ **Assessment:** Student assessment is addressed in the chosen electronic learning simulation.

_____ **Future:** As simulation is a rapidly expanding field of electronic technology, a view to the future of learning simulations (virtual reality) is maintained.

_____ **Ethics:** Ethical considerations of multisensory instruction is anticipated and supervised.

_____ **Software Selection:** Software selection procedures have been established that ensure teacher and community input.

Bibliography

The following books and articles have
been used in the construction
of this principal's handbook. Readers
are strongly encouraged to
explore the different references listed
in this bibliography.

Abramson, G. W. (1993). LinkWay Features and Design. *The Computing Teacher, 21*(2), 16–21.

Adams, D. M. and, M. Hamm (1987). *Electronic Learning: Issues and teaching ideas for educational computing, television, and visual literacy.* Springfield, IL: Charles C. Thomas.

Ambrose, D. W. (1991). The Effects of Hypermedia on Learning: A literature review. *Educational Technology, 31*(6), 51–55.

Anderson-Inman, L. (1994). Literacy Instruction in an Integrated Curriculum. *The Computing Teacher, 21*(4), 33–36.

Apple Computer, Inc. (1990). *Multimedia in Education: Tools for the way people learn.* Cupertino, CA: Apple Computer, Inc.

————. (1991). *Teaching, Learning & Technology: A planning guide.* Cupertino, CA: Apple Computer, Inc.

Armstrong, T. (1993). *Seven Kinds of Smart: Identifying and developing your many intelligences.* New York: Penguin Books.

Bailey, G. D. (ed.) (1993). *Computer-Based Integrated Learning Systems.* Englewood Cliffs, NJ: Educational Technology Publications.

Bailey, G. D., and G. L. Bailey (1994). *101 Activities for Creating Effective Technology Staff Development Programs: A sourcebook of games, stories, role playing and learning exercises for administrators.* New York: Scholastic.

Bailey, G. D., and D. Lumley (1994). *Technology Staff Development Programs: A leadership sourcebook for administrators.* New York: Scholastic.

Barker, J. A. (1992). *Future Edge: Discovering the new paradigms of success.* New York: William Morrow.

Bassett, E. (1992). New Technology for Video Conferences. *Electronic Learning, 11*(8), 20.

Bauer, D. G. (1994). *The Principal's Guide to Grant Success.* New York: Scholastic.

Becker, H. J. (1992). A Model for Improving Performance of Integrated Learning Systems: Mixed individualized/groups/whole class lessons, cooperative learning, and organizing time for teacher-led remediation of small groups. *Educational Technology, 32*(9), 6–15.

Bell, T. H., and D. L. Elmquist (1992). Technology: A catalyst for restructuring schools. *Electronic Learning, 11*(5), 10–11.

Bevilacqua, A. F. (1989). *Hypertext: Behind the hype.* ERIC Document Reproduction Service, No. 308 882.

Bittinger, A. (1991, June 11). Video Network to Connect Students in 7 schools. *Salina Journal, 1, 7.*

Bixler, B., and J. Spotts (1994). SCORE Courseware Offers Model for Adult Learners. *T.H.E. Journal, 21*(11), 76–79.

Boudrot, T. E., and C. A. Haugsness (1988). *Planning for Computer Instruction and*

Educational Technology: From district plans to building implementation. Topeka, KS: Kansas State Department of Education.

Bove, T., and C. Rhodes (1990). *Que's Macintosh Multimedia Handbook.* Carmel, IN: Que.

Bracey, G. W. (1988). The Impact of Computers. *Phi Delta Kappan, 70*(1), 70–74.

———. (1991). ILS Research Isn't Helpful. *Electronic Learning, 11*(1), 16.

———. (1992a). The Bright Future of Integrated Learning Systems. *Educational Technology, 32*(9), 60–62.

———. (1992b). Computers and Cooperative Learning. *Electronic Learning, 11*(5), 14.

———. (1992c). Creative Writing: Do word processors help or hurt students' creativity? *Electronic Learning, 12*(3), 12.

———. (1993). Assessing the New Assessments. *Principal, 72*(3), 34–36.

Branscum, D. (1992). Budget Computing. *MacWorld, 9*(11), 59–62.

Brewer, T. (1991). 10 Teacher Tips for Using Multimedia. *Electronic Learning, 10*(4), 14.

Bruce, C. (1992). Chip Bruce's Taxonomy of Educational Technology Applications. *The Holmes Group Forum, 6*(2), 10.

Bruder, I. (1989a). Distance Learning: What's holding back this boundless delivery system? *Electronic Learning, 8*(6), 30–35.

———. (1989b). Future Teachers: Are they prepared? *Electronic Learning, 8*(4), 32–39.

———. (1989c). New Ideas for Professional Development. *Electronic Learning, 9*(3), 22–28.

———. (1990). Restructuring Through Technology. Special supplement to *Business Week, No. 3191*, 32–38.

———. (1991). Distance Learning. *Electronic Learning, 11*(3), 20–28.

———. (1992a). Can Technology Help? *Electronic Learning, 12*(3), 18–19.

———. (1992b). What's New in Multimedia? *Electronic Learning, 12*(1), 16.

———. (1992c). What's New in Networks? *Electronic Learning, 12*(3), 14.

———. (1992d). Quantum Leap. *Electronic Learning, 12*(1), 22.

———. (1993). Alternative Assessment: Putting technology to the test. *Electronic Learning, 12*(4), 22–29.

Buchsbaum, H., M. Hill, and L. C. Orlando (1992). School Reform: Why you need technology to get there. *Electronic Learning, 11*(8), 22–28.

Buerry, K., B. Haslan, and D. Legters (1990). Images of Potential: From vision to reality. Special reprint from *Business Week, No. 3191*, 50–53.

Burry, K. (1993). The Earth Day Treasure Hunt: Using online resources as a research tool. *The Computing Teacher, 21*(1), 53–54.

Bush, V. (1945). The Way We May Think. *The Atlantic, 176*(1), 101–108.

Butzin, S. M. (1992). Project CHILD: A new twist on integrated learning systems. *T.H.E. Journal, 20(2)*, 90–94.

Cawelti, G. (1991). Clarifying the Means and Ends of Restructuring. *Update: ASCD, 33(8)*, 2.

Center for Children and Technology: Bank Street College (1990). *Application in Educational Assessment: Future technologies*. ERIC Document Reproduction Service, No. 340 773.

Center for Learning Technologies (1984). *Getting Started: Planning and implementing computer instruction in schools*. Albany, NY: Center for Learning Technologies.

Cetron, M., and M. Gayle (1991). *Educational Renaissance: Our schools at the turn of the twenty-first century*. New York: St. Martin's Press.

Collins, A. (1991a). Cognitive Apprenticeship and Instructional Technology. In L. Idon and B. F. Jones (eds.) *Educational Values and Cognitive Instruction: Implications for reform* (121–138). Hillsdale, NJ: Lawrence Erlbaum Associates.

————. (1991b). The Role of Computer Technology in Restructuring Schools. *Phi Delta Kappan, 73(1)*, 28–36.

Cringely, R. X. (1992). Welcome to the Future. *Success, 39(7)*, 22–28.

Cuban, L. (1988). *The Managerial Imperative: The practice of leadership in schools*. Albany, NY: State University of New York Press.

Cuban, L. (1992). Computers Meet Classroom: Classroom wins. *Education Week, 12(10)*, 36–7.

Daggett, W. R. (1989). *The Changing Nature of Work—A challenge to education*. Speech to Kansas Legislators, October, 1989.

Daiute, C. (1992). Multimedia Computer: Extending the resource of kindergarten to writers across the grades. *Language Arts, 69(4)*, 250–260.

David, J. L. (1989). Synthesis of Research on School-Based Management. *Educational Leadership, 46(8)*, 45–53.

————. (1991). Restructuring with Technology. *Phi Delta Kappan, 73(1)*, 28–36.

Dede, C. (1987). Empowering Environments, Hypermedia and Microworlds. *The Computing Teacher, 15(3)*, 20–24.

————. (1988). The Role of Hypertext in Transforming Information into Knowledge. NECC Conference, Dallas, TX, 1988.

————. (1989a). The Evolution of Information Technology: Implications for curriculum. *Educational Leadership, 47(1)*, 23–26.

————. (1989b). Planning Guidelines for Emerging Instructional Technologies. *Educational Technology, 29(4)*, 7–12.

————. (1992). Making the Most of Multimedia. The Electronic School, Special supplement to the *American School Board Journal, 178(9)*, A13–A15.

Delaney, B. (1994). Virtual Reality Lands the Job. *New Media, 4*(8), 40–48.

Demming, W. E. (1986). *Out of the Crisis.* Cambridge, MA: Massachusetts Institute of Technology.

Dervarics, C. (1991a). Learning Systems Even the Odds. *Executive Educator, 13*(10), Special supplement, "The Electronic School: Innovative Uses of Technology in Education," A21–A22.

————. (1991b). Technology Speeds School Restructuring. *Executive Educator, 13*(10), Special supplement, "The Electronic School: Innovative Uses of Technology in Education," A19–A21.

Dickinson, D. (1992). Multiple Technologies for Multiple Intelligences. The Electronic School, Special supplement to the *American School Board Journal, 178*(9), A8–A12.

D'Ignazio, F. (1988). Bringing the 1990s to the Classroom of Today. *Phi Delta Kappan, 71*(4), 25–31.

————. (1989a). Multimedia on Wheels. *The Computing Teacher, 17*(2), 24–27.

————. (1989b). Welcome to the Multimedia Sandbox. *The Computing Teacher, 19*(3), 27–28.

————. (1989–90). Through the Looking Glass: The multiple layers of multimedia. *The Computing Teacher, 17*(4), 25–31.

———— (1990a). Electronic Highways and the Classroom of the Future. *The Computing Teacher, 17*(8), 20–24.

————. (1990b). An Inquiry Centered Classroom of the Future. *The Computing Teacher, 17*(6), 16–19.

———— (1990c). Multimedia Copyright. *The Computing Teacher, 17*(5), 32–35.

———— (1990d). Multimedia Horsepower: How much is enough? *The Computing Teacher, 17*(7), 16–18.

———— (1990e). Multimedia Training Centers: The highest tech at affordable prices. *The Computing Teacher, 18*(2), 54–55.

———— (1991a). Scavenged Inquiry Centers: Multimedia learning on wheels. Packet from author.

———— (1991b). Integrating the Work Environment of the 1990's into Today's CLassrooms. *T.H.E. Journal, 18* (11), 95.

———— (1991c). A New Curriculum Paradigm: The fusion of technology, the arts, and classroom instruction. *The Computing Teacher, 18*(2), 54.

———— (1992a). Getting a Jump on the Future. *Electronic Learning, 12*(3), 28–31.

———— (1992b). Toward a Collaborative Environment. *T.H.E. Journal,* Special multimedia supplement, 34.

————. (1992c). Restructuring Knowledge: Opportunities for classroom learning in the 1990's. *The Computing Teacher, 18*(1), 22–25.

Droegemueller, L. (1991). *Distance Learning: A plan for telecommunications in Kansas.* Topeka, KS: Kansas State Department of Education.

Economist (1991). Television in Schools: Pupils or consumers? Channel one offers current affairs and advertisements aimed at high school students. *Economist, 319 (7705),* 31.

Edwards, L. D. (1994). Educational Technology Research Section: Mathematical explorations in LOGO: Report of a pilot student from Costa Rica. *Educational Technology, 34*(5), 56–60.

Eiser, L. (1990). A Guide to Telecommunication Services. *Technology & Learning, 11*(3), 36–43.

Electronic Learning (1991). Integrated Learning Systems: How to buy an ILS. *Electronic Learning,* Special supplement, Winter, 1991.

———. (1992a). ILS Vendors Embrace the MAC. *Electronic Learning, 11*(6), Special edition.

———. (1992b). The Most Complete Guide Ever to Telecommunications. *Electronic Learning, 11*(6),18–27.

———. (1993). Networks: Learning beyond the classroom. *Electronic Learning, 12*(7), Special edition, 6.

English, W. E., and J. C. Hill (1990). *Restructuring: The principal and curriculum change.* Reston, VA: National Association of Secondary School Principals.

Farley, C. J. (1991, September 18). Virtual Reality Is Computer's Flying Carpet. *USA Today,* pp. 1D and 2D.

Finkel, L. (1990). Moving Your District Toward Technology: It's a bit easier now that we know many of the don'ts! *School Administrator,* Special issue, 35–37.

———. (1992a). Are ILSes Worth the $$? *Electronic Learning, 12*(1), 18.

———. (1992b). What Does a Curriculum Director Do with Technology? *Electronic Learning, 11*(8), 16.

Fullan, M. G., and Stiegelbauer, S. (1991). *The New Meaning of Educational Change,* 2nd ed. New York: Teachers College Press.

Gardner, H. (1983). *Frames of Mind: The theory of multiple intelligences.* New York: Basic Books.

———. (1988). Mobilizing Resources for Individual-Centered Learning. In R. S. Nickerson and P. Zodhiates (eds.), *Technology in Education: Looking toward 2020,* (pp. 25–42). Hillsdale, NJ: Lawrence Erlbaum Associates.

Gathany, N. C., and J. K. Stehr-Green (1994). Putting Life into Computer-Based Training: The creation of an epidemiologic case study. *Educational Technology, 34*(6), 44–47.

Gibbon, S. Y., Jr. (1987). Learning and Instruction in the Information Age. In M.A. White (ed.) *What Curriculum for the Information Age?* (pp. 1–23), Hillsdale, NJ: Lawrence Erlbaum Associates.

Gill, E. K. (1992). High Voltage PCs. *Presentations, 6*(9), 25–30.

Goldberg, C. J. (1992). LCD Panels Team with Projectors. *MacWeek, 6*(21), 27–30.

Goodlad, J. L. (1984). *A Place Called School: Prospects for the future.* New York: McGraw-Hill.

Gore, A. (1990). The Digitization of Schools. Special reprint from *Business Week, No. 3191,* 28–30.

————. (1991, January-February). Information Superhighways: The next information revolution. *Futurist,* 21–23.

Graumann, P. (1994). GALAXY Classroom: Television for tomorrow. *Technology & Learning, 14*(7), 34–38.

Grunwald, P. (1991). Telecommunications in the Classroom. Special supplement to *The Executive Educator, 13*(10), A4–A11.

Handy, C. (1990). *The Age of Unreason.* Boston: Harvard Business School Papers.

Hargadon, T. (1992). Communications Medium. *New Media, 2*(11), 29.

Harris, J. (1994). People-to-People: Projects on the Internet. *The Computing Teacher, 21*(4), 48–52.

Helsel, S. K. (1990). *Interactive Optical Technologies in Education and Training.* Westport, CT: Meckler.

————. (1992). Virtual Reality as a Learning Medium. *Instructional Delivery Systems, 6*(4), 4–5.

Helsel, S. K., and J. P. Roth (eds.)(1991). *Virtual Reality: Theory, practice and promise.* Westport, CT: Meckler.

Henderson, J. (1991). Designing Realities: Interactive media, virtual realities and cyberspace. In S. K. Helsel and J. P. Roth (eds.), *Virtual Reality: Theory, practice and promise* (65–73). Westport, CT: Meckler.

Hertzke, E. R. (1992). The Administrator's Role in Adopting and Using Integrated Learning Systems. *Educational Technology, 32*(9), 44–45.

Higgins, J. (1990). Electronic Schools and American Competitiveness. Special reprint from *Business Week, No. 3191,* 8–10.

Hill, M. (1992a). The New Literacy. *Electronic Learning, 12*(1) 28–33.

————. (1992b). What's New in Virtual Reality. *Electronic Learning, 12*(2), 10.

————. (1992c). Writing to Learning: Processing writing moves into the curriculum. *Electronic Learning, 12*(3), 20–27.

————. (1993a). Blackboard-Disk Jockeys. *Electronic Learning,* Special Edition, 16–17.

————. (1993b). What's New in ILSes? *Electronic Learning, 12*(4), 12.

Hodgkinson, H. (1991a). Reform Versus Reality. *Phi Delta Kappan, 73*(1), 9–17.

————. (1991b). Today's Curriculum: How appropriate will it be in the year 2000? *NASSP Bulletin, 75*(535), 2–7.

Holzberg, C. S. (1994). Technology in Special Education. *Technology & Learning, 14*(7), 18–21.

Hooper, S., and M. J. Hannafin (1991). Psychological Perspectives on Emerging Instructional Technologies: A critical analysis. *Educational Psychologist, 26*(1), 69–95.

Hughes, L. (1992). Gaining Fluency. *Educational Computing & Technology, 13*(8), 33–34.

Hutchins, C. (1993). Lights Cameras...Students. *Electronic Learning, 13*(2), 30.

Jacobson, P. (1992). Save the Cities! *SimCity* in Grade 2–5. *The Computing Teacher, 20*(2), 14–15.

Jancich, H. S. (1991). The Evolution of a Revolution: Technology in the classroom. *The Balance Sheet, 73*(1), 19–21.

Johnson, D. W., and R. T. Johnson (1985). Cooperative Learning: One key to computer assisted learning. *The Computing Teacher, 13*(1), 11–13.

———. (1991). *Learning Together and Alone: Cooperative, competitive and individualistic learning.* Englewood Cliffs, NJ: Prentice Hall.

Johnston, J. (1985). Information Literacy: Academic skills for a new age. *National Institute of Education, September, 1985,* 3–18.

Johnson, R. (1991). *Leading Business Teams: How teams can use technology and group process tools to enhance performance.* Reading, MA: Addison-Wesley.

Jonassen, D. H. (1986). Hypertext Principles for Text and Courseware Design. *Educational Psychologist, 21*(4), 269–292.

———. (1989). *Hypertext/Hypermedia.* Englewood Cliffs, NJ: Educational Technology Publications.

———. (1991). Thinking Technology: Context is everything. *Educational Technology, 31*(6), 35–37.

———. (1992). Learning vs. Information. *Journal of Educational Multimedia and Hypermedia, 1*(1), 3–5.

Jordahl, G. (1991). Breaking Down Classroom Walls: Distance learning comes of age. *Technology & Learning, 11*(5), 72–78.

Kansas State Department of Education (1989). *Kansas Schools for the 21st Century.* Topeka, KS: Author.

Kaplan-Neher, A. (1989). New Media: Dymystifying the technology. *Syllabus, No. 7,* 2–8.

Kay, A. C. (1991). Computers, Networks and Education. *Scientific American, 265*(3), 138–148.

Knirk, F. G. (1992). Facility Requirements for Integrated Learning Systems. *Educational Technology, 32*(9), 26–32.

Koeppel, D. L. (1991). Why Channel One May Be Here to Stay. *Marketing Week, 32*(23), 22–23.

Komoski, K. (1990). Integrated Learning Systems Take Integrated Efforts. *School Administrator,* Special issue, 1990, 25–27.

Kuhn, T. S. (1962). *The Structure of Scientific Revolutions.* Chicago: University of Chicago Press.

Lantz, E. (1992). Virtual Reality in Science Museums. *Instructional Delivery Systems, 6*(4), 10–12.

Leslie, J. (1993). Kids Connecting. *Wired, 1*(5), 90–93.

Lezotte, L. W. (1989). School Improvement Based on Effective Schools Research. In D. K. Lispky, and A. Gartner (eds.), *Beyond Separate Education: Quality education for all.* (25–35). Baltimore: P. H. Brookes.

————. (1991). School Improvement Based on Effective Schools Research: The decade ahead. *Educational Considerations, 18*(2), 19–21.

Lindroth, L. K. (1994). Lights, Action, Math. *Electronic Learning, 13*(7), 42–43.

Lipson, S. B. (1992). 10 Base T-hubs: Stars on the ethernet horizon. *MacUser, 8*(10), 25–40.

Lumley, D., and G. D. Bailey (1990). Integrated Learning Systems: A new method of delivering effective instruction. *Kansas Journal of Educational Technology, 1*(1), 5–6.

————. (1993). *Planning for Technology: A guidebook for school administrators.* New York: Scholastic.

Maddux, C. D., and J. W. Willis (1992). Integrated Learning Systems and Their Alternatives: Problems and cautions. *Educational Technology, 32*(9), 51–57.

Mageau, T. (1990). ILS: Its new role in schools. *Electronic Learning, 10*(1), 22–32.

————. (1991). Redefining the Textbook. *Electronic Learning, 10*(5), 14–18.

————. (1992). Integrating an ILS: Two teaching models that work. *Electronic Learning, 11*(4), 16–22.

Male, M. (1986). Cooperative Learning for Effective Mainstreaming. *The Computing Teacher, 14*(1), 35–37.

Marchionini, G. (1988). Hypermedia and Learning: Freedom and chaos. *Educational Technology, 28*(11), 8–12.

Marshall, G. (1990). Drill Won't Do. *American School Board Journal, 177*(7), 21–23.

McCarthy, M. J. (1991). *Mastering the Information Age: A course in working smarter, thinking better, and learning faster.* Los Angles, CA: Jeremy P. Tarcher.

McCarthy, R. (1992). Hands on Math and Science. *Electronic Learning, 12*(1), 9–13.

McCarthy, R., and M. Revenaugh (1989). For Basic Skills Instruction: Integrated learning systems represent a package that won't bite. *Electronic Learning,* Special supplement, 13–17.

McCarty, P. (1991). Bringing the World into the Classroom. *Principal, 71*(2), 8–10.

McKinney, B. C. (1991). The Virtual World of HDTV. In S. K. Helsel and J. P. Roth (eds.), *Virtual Reality: Theory, practice and promise*, (41–49). Westport, CT: Meckler.

McLellan, H. (1991). Virtual Environments and Situated Learning. *Multimedia Review, fall, 1991*, 30–37.

McLuhan, M. (1962). *The Gutenberg Galaxy: The making of typographic man.* Toronto: University of Toronto Press.

McREL (1990). *National Education Goals: Can they lead to real reform?* Aurora, CO: McREL.

———. (1992a). Having Computers Is Step One: New schools need to reach out to telecommunications networks. *Research Roundup*, November, 3.

———. (1992b). Technologies Help Teachers Overcome Time, Space Barriers and Make Communication Easier. *Research Roundup*, November, 1.

Mecklenberger, J. A. (1990). The New Revolution. Special reprint *Business Week, No. 3191*, 22–26.

Meeks, B. (1991). Computers for Communication. In J. Rutkowska and C. Crook (eds.), *Computers, Cognition and Development* (55–67). Los Angles, CA: Jeremy P. Tarcher.

Microsoft Press (1991). *Computer Dictionary.* Redmond, WA: Microsoft Press.

Miles, S. (1991). Project 2000: Surrattsville High School Model Telecommunications and School Restructuring: An interactive videoconference presented by the National School Board Association, October 31, 1991.

Mill, H. (1988). *An Administrator's Manual for the Use of Microcomputers in the Schools.* Englewood Cliffs, NJ: Prentice Hall.

Minnesota Department of Education (1990a). *Desktop Multimedia in the Classroom.* St. Paul, MN: Minnesota Department of Education.

———. (1990b). *Hypermedia in the Classroom.* St. Paul, MN: Minnesota Department of Education (videotape).

Mojkowski, C. (1990). 10 Essential Truths to Help You Plan for Technology Use. *Tech Trends, 30*(7), 18–22.

Molnar, A. R. (1990). Computers in Education: A historical perspective of the unfinished task. *T.H.E. Journal, 18*(4), 80–83.

Morehouse, D. E., and S. H. Stockdill (1992). Technology Adoption Model. *Educational Technology, 32(2),* 57–59.

Morehouse, D. L., M. L. Hoaglund, and R. H. Schmidt (1987). Interactive Television Findings, Issues and Recommendations: An analysis based on evaluation of Minnesota's Technology Demonstration Program. Unpublished, Feb. 1, 1987.

Morse, R. H. (1991). Computer Uses in Secondary Science Education. *ERIC Digest, EDO-1R-91-1,* 1–2.

Motorola Codex (1992). *The Basics Book of Information Networking.* Reading, MA: Addison-Wesley.

Muller, D. G., and R. Leonetti (1992). A Major Technological Advancement in Training. *Instructional Delivery Systems, 6(4),* 15–17.

Mulvey, W. (1991). The Dynamics of Telepublishing, Telecommunications and School Restructuring: An interactive videoconference presented by the National School Board Association, October 31, 1991.

Nadler, G., and S. Hibino (1990). *Breakthrough Thinking: Why we must change the way we solve problems and the seven principles to achieve this.* Rocklin, CA: Prima Publishing.

Naisbitt, J., and P. Aburdene (1990). *Megatrends 2000: Ten new directions for the 1990's.* New York: Avon Books.

National Commission on Excellence in Education (1983). *A Nation at Risk: The imperative for educational reform.* Washington, DC: U.S. Government Printing Office.

National Education Goals Panel (1991). *The National Educational Goals Report: Building a nation of learners.* Washington, DC: National Education Goals Panel.

Nelson, T. (1987). *Computer Lib/Dream Machines.* Redmond, WA: Tempus Books.

Newhard, R. (1987). Converting Information into Knowledge: The promise of CD-ROM. *Wilson Library Bulletin, 62*(4), 36–38.

Newman, D. (1992). Technology as Support for School Structure and School Restructuring. *Phi Delta Kappan, 74*(4), 308–315.

Newman, F. M. (1991). Linking Restructuring to Authentic Student Achievement. *Phi Delta Kappan, 72*(6), 458–463.

Nix, D. (1990). Should Computers Know What You Can Do with Them? In D. Nix and R. J. Spiro (eds.), *Cognition, Education and Multimedia: Exploring ideas in high technology* (143–162). Hillsdale, NJ: Lawrence Erlbaum Associates.

Nix, D., and R. Spiro (eds.) (1990). *Cognition, Educational Multimedia: Exploring ideas in high technology.* Hillsdale, NJ: Lawrence Erlbaum Associates.

Novelli, J. (1993). Better Tools for Better Teamwork. *Instructor, 103*(3), 43–45.

November, A. (1992a). Brave New World Revisited? *Electronic Learning, 11*(6), 50.

———. (1992b). Enabling Teachers to Become Researchers. *Electronic Learning, 11*(8), 58.

———. (1992c). Familyware. *Electronic Learning, 11*(7), 50.

———. (1992d). The Promised Land: Looking to Moses for a lesson on restructuring. *Electronic Learning, 12*(1), 20.

Ohlson, K. J., and A. Michael (1992). LocalTalking in LAN Land: A glossary. *MacUser, 8*(10), 45–50.

Olson, G., and D. E. Atkins (1990). Supporting Collaboration with Advances in Multimedia Electronic Mail: The National Science Foundation. EXPRESS project. In J. Galegher, R. E. Kraut, and C. Egido (eds.), *Intellectual Teamwork:*

Social and technological foundation of cooperative work (429–451). Hillsdale, NJ: Lawrence Erlbaum Associates.

Papert, S. (1980). *Mindstorms: Children, computers, and powerful ideas.* New York: Basic Books.

————. (1984). New Theories for New Learnings. *School Psychology Review, 13*(4), 422–428.

————. (1993). The Children's Machine: Rethinking school in the age of the computer. New York: Basic Books.

Papert, S., and I. Herel (eds.)(1990). *Constructionism.* Norwood, NJ: Albex.

Pea, R. D. (1984). Beyond Amplification: Using the computer to reorganize mental functioning. *Education Psychologist, 13*(4), 168–182.

Pearlman, R. (1989). Technology's Role in Restructuring Schools. *Electronic Learning, 8*(8), 8–14.

————. (1991). Restructuring with Technology: A tour of schools where it's happening. *Technology & Learning, 11*(4), 30–37.

Perelman, L. J. (1988). Restructuring the System Is the Solution. *Phi Delta Kappan, 70*(1), 20–24.

————. (1990a). Change Equals Choice Plus Technology: Without both, schools are headed for history's scrapheap. *Teacher Magazine, October,* 59–60.

————. (1990b). A New Learning Enterprise. *Business Week, No. 3191,* Special supplement, 10–20.

————. (1992). *School's Out: Hyperlearning, the new technology, and the end of education.* New York: William Morrow.

Pettacia, T. (1993). Making Connections. *MacUser, 9*(2), 100–106.

Pritchard, W. H., and J. D. Busby (1991). A Blueprint for Successfully Integrating Technology into Your Institution. *T.H.E. Journal,* Macintosh special issue, 48–52.

Privateer, P. M., and C. MacCrate (1992). Odyssey Project: A search for new learning solutions. *T.H.E. Journal, 20*(3), 76–80.

Provenzo, E. F., Jr. (1986). *Beyond the Gutenberg Galaxy: Microcomputers and the emergence of the post-typographic culture.* New York: Teachers College Press.

Ravitch, D. (1987). Technology and the Curriculum: Promise and peril. In M. A. White (ed.), *What Curriculum for the Information Age?* (25–39) Hillsdale, NJ: Lawrence Erlbaum Associates.

Ray, D. (1989). Administrators Have a Crucial Role to Play in Transforming Education. *Electronic Learning, 8*(4), 6–8.

————. (1992). Educational Technology Leadership for the Age of Restructuring. *The Computing Teacher, 9*(6), 8–14.

Reich, R. B. (1991). *The Work of Nations: Preparing ourselves for 21st century capitalism.* New York: Alfred A. Knopf.

Reissman, R. (1992). A Biosphere Research Expedition. *The Computing Teacher, 20*(1), 30–32.

Reveaux, T. (1992). Virtual Reality Gets Real. *New Media, 3*(1), 32–33.

Rezabek, R. A. (1989). *Elaborated Resources: An instructional design strategy for hypermedia.* ERIC Document Reproduction Service, No. 316 175.

Rist, M. (1991). Whittling Away at Public Education. *The Executive Educator, 13*(9), 22–28.

Rockman, S., and K. Lillenthal (1992). Today's Distance Learning. *Inventing Tomorrow's Schools, 2*(1), 5–6.

Ross, T. W. (1992). A Principal's Guide to ILS Facilities Installation. *Educational Technology, 32*(9), 33–35.

Ruthven, K. (1985). Theory into Practice. In D. J. Smith (ed.), *Information Technology in Education: Signposts and research directions,* (21–30). London: Economics and Social Research Council.

Sarason, S. B. (1990). *The Predictable Failure of Educational Reform: Can we change course before it's too late?* San Francisco: Jossey-Bass Publishers.

Schneiner, B. (1993). Data Guardians: How strong are the software locks on 24 security products? *MacWorld, 19*(2), 145–151.

Schrage, M. (1990). *Shared Minds: The new technologies of collaboration.* New York: Random House.

Schwartz, J. L. (1987). Closing the Gap Between Education and Schools. In M. A. White (ed.), *What Curriculum for the Information Age?* (67–75). Hillsdale, NJ: Lawrence Erlbaum Associates.

Secretary's Commission on Achieving Necessary Skills, U.S. Department of Labor (1991). *What Work Requires of Schools.* Washington, DC: U.S. Government Printing Office.

Senge, P. M. (1990). *The Fifth Discipline: The art & practice of the learning organization.* New York: Doubleday.

Sergiovanni, T. J. (1989). Value Driven Schools. In J. J. Walberg and J. J. Lane (eds.), *Organizing for Learning: Toward the 21st century* (31-41). Reston, VA: National Association of Secondary School Principals.

Sheingold, K. (1991). Restructuring for Learning with Technology: The potential for synergy. *Phi Delta Kappan, 73*(1), 17–27.

Sheingold, K., and M. S. Tucker (eds.) (1990). *Restructuring for Learning with Technology.* New York: Center for Technology in Education and the National Center on Education and the Economy.

Shepard, L. A. (1991). Psychometricians' Beliefs about Learning. *Educational Researcher, 20*(7), 2–11.

Sherry, M. (1990a). Implementing an Integrated Instructional System: Critical issues. *Phi Delta Kappan, 72*(2), 118–120.

———. (1990b). Integrated Learning Systems: An EPIE Institute Report: Integrated Instructional Systems. *T.H.E. Journal, 18*(2), 86–89.

———. (1991). The Future of Integrated Learning Systems. *Inventing Tomorrow's Schools, 1*(1), 6.

———. (1992a). Integrated Learning Systems: What may we expect in the future? *Educational Technology, 32*(9), 58–59.

———. (1992b). How much does an ILS cost? *Electronic Learning, 11*(6), 8.

Shockley, H. A. (1992). Turkey or Turnkey? Integrating an Integrated Learning System. *Educational Technology, 32*(9), 22–25.

Shore, A., and M. F. Johnson (1992). Integrated Learning Systems: A vision for the future. *Educational Technology, 32*(9), 36–39.

Sizer, T. R. (1991). No Pain, No Gain. *Educational Leadership, 48*(8), 32–34.

———. (1992a). The Bigger Picture: Setting high standards with the help of technology. *Electronic Learning, 12(*2), 50.

———. (1992b). Diverse Practice, Shared Ideas: The essential school. In J. J. Walberg and J. J. Lane (eds.), *Organizing for Learning: Toward the 21st century* (1–8). Reston, VA: National Association of Secondary School Principals.

———. (1992c). *Horace's School: Redesigning the American high school.* New York: Houghton Mifflin.

Slavin, R. E. (1983). *Cooperative Learning.* New York: Longman.

———. (1989a). PET and the Pendulum: Faddism in education and how to stop it. *Phi Delta Kappan, 70*(10), 752–758.

———. (1989b). Reading Effects of IBM's "Writing to Read" Program: A review of evaluations. *Education, Evaluation and Policy Analysis, 13*(1), 1–11.

Solomon, G. (1993). The Student Maestro. *Electronic Learning, 13*(1), 24–25.

Southwest Plains Regional Service Center (1989). 2-Way Visually Interactive Instructional Television Network. Paper presented at the Kansas Association of School Boards Technology in Education Conference, Topeka, Kansas.

Spiro, R. J., and J. C. Jehng (1990). Cognitive Flexibility and Hypertext: Theory and technology for nonlinear and multidimensional transversal of complex subject matter. In D. Nix and R. J. Spiro (eds.), *Cognition, Education and Multimedia: Exploring ideas in high technology* (162–205). Hillsdale, NJ: Lawrence Erlbaum Associates.

St. Clair, R. (1989). An Information Age School. In H. J. Walberg and J. J. Lane (eds.), *Organizing for Learning: Toward the 21st century,* (66–71). Reston, VA: National Association of Secondary School Principals.

Stanton, M., and W. Wilson (1992). Making the Most of Cable Television Technology. *T.H.E. Journal, 19(*10), 66–68.

Steller, A. (1989). One Model for Effective Educational Reform. In H. J. Walberg and J. J. Lane (eds.), *Organizing for Learning: Toward the 21st century,* (21–30). Reston, VA: National Association of Secondary School Principals.

Sterns, H. S. (1993). History Comes Alive. *Electronic Learning,* Special Editions, 8–9.

Taylor, J. (1992). Safeguarding Computer Equipment. The Electronic School, Special supplement to the *American School Board Journal, 178*(9), A27–A34.

Tiene, D. (1993). Channel One: Good or bad news for our schools? *Educational Leadership, 50*(8), 46–51.

Toffler, A. (1970). *Future Shock.* New York: Random House.

——. (1980). *Third Wave.* New York: William Morrow.

——. (1990). *Power Shift: Knowledge, wealth and violence at the edge of the 21st century.* New York: Bantam Books.

Traub, D. C. (1991). Simulated World as Classroom: The potential for designed learning within virtual environments. In S. K. Helsel, and J. P. Roth (eds.), *Virtual Reality: Theory, practice and promise,* (111–121). Westport, CT: Meckler.

Trotter, A. (1990a). Computer Learning. *American School Board Journal, 177*(7), 12–18.

——. (1990b). Buying Trouble. *American School Board Journal, 177*(7), 16–18.

——. (1991). Are Today's Kids Having Too Much Fun in Your Classrooms? *Executive Educator, 13*(6), 20–24.

Tucker, M. (1992). The Genie in the Bottle. *Electronic Learning, 12*(3), 50.

Tyre, T. (1992). Jostens Learning Interactive Media: The ultimate ILS delivers networked video. *T.H.E. Journal, 20*(1), 14–15.

Tyson, H., and A. Woodward (1989). Why Students Aren't Learning Very Much From Textbooks. *Educational Leadership, 47*(3), 14–17.

U. S. Congress, Office of Technology Assessment (1988). *Power On!: New tools for teaching and learning.* Washington, DC: U.S. Government Printing Office.

——. (1989). *Linking for Learning: A new course for education.* Washington, DC: U.S. Government Printing Office.

U. S. Department of Labor: Secretary's Commission on Achieving Necessary Skills. (1991). *What Work Requires of Schools: A SCANS report on America 2000.* Washington, DC: U.S. Government Printing Office.

Van Dam, A. (1988). Hypertext '87 Keynote Address. *Comm. ACM, 31*(7), 887–895.

van den Brink, J. (1994). Outside, a World Goes By...Applying Mathematics with Flight Simulators. *The Computing Teacher, 21*(5), 21–32.

Vandergrif, K. E., M. Kemper, S. Champion, and J. A. Hannigan (1987). CD-ROM: An emerging technology: Part 2: Planning and management strategies. *School Library Journal, 33*(8), 22–25.

Van Dusen, L. M., and Worthen, B. R. (1992). Factors that Facilitate or Impede Implementation of Integrated Learning Systems. *Educational Technology, 32*(9), 16–21.

Van Horn, R. (1991). Educational Power Tools: New instructional delivery systems. *Phi Delta Kappan, 72*(7), 527–533.

Walberg, H. J., and J. J. Lane (eds.) (1989). *Organizing for Learning: Toward the 21st century*. Reston, VA: National Association of Secondary School Principals.

Ward, A. (1991a). Restructuring Elementary Education. Special supplement to the *Executive Educator, 13*(10), A24–A25.

———. (1991b). What Place Does Technology Deserve in Education? Special supplement to the *Executive Educator, 13*(10), A14–A15.

———. (1992). A Brave New Information World. The Electronic School, Supplement to the *American School Board Journal, 178*(9), A16–A18.

Weisberg, L. (1992). Beyond Drills and Practice in a One Computer Classroom. *The Computing Teacher, 20*(1), 27–28.

Whisler, J. S. (1988). Distance Learning Technologies: An aid to restructuring schools. In *Noteworthy*, Mid-Continent Regional Regional Educational Laboratory (28–41). Washington, DC: U.S. Government Printing Office.

White, M. A. (ed.) (1983). *The Future of Electronic Learning*. Hillsdale, NJ: Lawrence Erlbaum Associates.

———. (1986). Implication of the Technologies for Human Learning. *Peabody Journal of Education, 64*(1), 155–169.

———. (1987a). Information and Imagery Education. In M. A. White (ed.) *What Curriculum for the Information Age?* (41–66). Hillsdale, NJ: Lawrence Erlbaum Associates.

———. (ed.) (1987b). *What Curriculum for the Information Age?* Hillsdale, NJ: Lawrence Erlbaum Associates.

———. (1989a). Current Trends in Education and Technology as Signs to the Future. *Education & Computing, 5,* 3–10.

———. (1989b). Educators Must Ask Themselves Some Important Questions. *Electronic Learning, 9*(1),6–8.

———. (1991). Images Foster Greater Learning. *Electronic Learning, 11*(1), 6.

———. (1992). Are ILSs Good Education? *Educational Technology, 32*(9), 49–50.

Wigley, G. (1988) Telecommunications in the Classroom: Telecommunications planning guide for educators. *The Computing Teacher, 16*(3), 24–29.

Wilder, G. Z., and M. Fowles (1992). Assessing the Outcomes of Computer-Based Instruction: The experience of Maryland. *T.H.E. Journal, 20*(2), 82–84.

Wilson, J. (1990). Integrated Learning Systems: A primer. *Classroom Computer Learning, 10*(5), 22–36.

Wilson, T. (1991). Here's What's on the School Technology Horizon. Special supplement to the *Executive Educator, 13(10),* A11–A13.

Wood, C., and R. Melville (1992). Consumer Watch: National guide to user groups. *PC World, 10*(10), 31–44.

Zorfass, J., and A. R. Remz (1992). Successful Technology Integration: The role of communication and collaboration. *Middle School Journal, 23*(5), 39–43.